**CORRINNE
ARMOUR**

**ANNELI
BLUNDELL**

Developing
Direct Reports

Taking the guesswork out
of leading leaders

Bacca House Press, Melbourne Australia
Developing Direct Reports: Taking the guesswork
out of leading leaders
Corrinne Armour, Anneli Blundell and Belinda Cohen

ISBN: 978-0-9942601-1-6

Edited by Cavalletti Communications
Cover & Interior Design by Logo Pogo

Published in Australia by Bacca House Press.
First Edition

Bacca House Press

About the Authors

Corrinne Armour

Waging a war on wasted potential, Corrinne's mission is empower leaders and teams to get out of their own way and embrace 'fearless leadership'. Known for her innovative approach, results focus and the ability to tell it like it is, she is recognised as a provoker of change and growth.

After living in Asia for a few years, Corrinne cooks a mean curry.

Anneli Blundell

As a professional 'people whisperer', Anneli has been working with leaders and teams to improve their communication and interpersonal intelligence for almost a decade. She brings to her clients a recognised expertise in the field of 'below conscious communication' and motivation and is obsessed with decoding people and performance dynamics for improved results.

Anneli also rates herself as an excellent parallel parker.

Belinda Cohen

Performance improvement is at the heart of all Belinda's work. With a natural curiosity for what drives behavioural diversity, Belinda brings a non-judgmental, supportive and 'no excuses' approach to her clients. She combines her legal and leadership experience with her passion for helping people work smarter. Belinda assists her clients to simplify the complex to bring about fresh perspectives and a new focus.

Belinda's ability to plan and book travel of any kind is an enviable skill.

All three are accomplished speakers, trainers and mentors. Together, they have published two other specialist reference books on shifting human behaviour. They are all passionate about their family, the privilege of doing great work with wonderful clients and quality dark chocolate.

Testimonials

"Wow — you can't help but be a better leader after reading this book. But more importantly, this book will give you the savvy to develop leadership in others. Deeply insightful and incredibly practical — an essential primer for any leader of leaders looking to develop the leaders of tomorrow."

– Dr Jason Fox, bestselling author of The Game Changer

"One of the challenges for executives in senior leadership roles is the significant investment of time spent on managing people issues and growing the next generation of leaders. And yet few executives are trained in the basics of psychology to help navigate through difficult people issues and know the best interventions to help grow their people.

'Developing Direct Reports' is a life line for any executive who can clearly see the impact of their direct reports' behaviour, but is unsure what to do. The book provides practical advice on how to diagnose leadership derailers and simple coaching tips to effectively develop people.

For those executives brave enough to hold up the mirror and assess one's own behaviours, 'Developing Direct Reports' is also a valuable tool for their own leadership development."

– Chris Akayan, Group General Manager - Human Resources, Mirvac

"Developing Direct Reports is so much more than just another leadership toolbox. It's a flight-path for any leader who wants to effectively forecast, navigate and enjoy the complexities and opportunities which leading any team entails. There's both laughter and solemn recognition to be had in reflecting on the 12 Leadership Derailers, which forms an inspirational platform for a key takeaway: that leadership is a privilege we should never take for granted."

– Sean Hughes, Senior Executive

"This book takes an enigmatically practical approach: a readable deep-dive into self-awareness, team-awareness and the neuroscience of leadership … balanced by practical step-by-step checklists anyone can follow. In our complex, changing world, knowing how to work with people and issues and "discover, decode and design" solutions is vital. The practical coaching tips included can be applied to any of the 12 leadership "derailer" behaviours that will be all-too-familiar to new and experienced leaders alike. Government, business, social sector: people are people and have shared subconscious drivers and concerns: and almost every interpersonal contingency is addressed. This book should form part of the library of every manager: either as a quick-check refresher for senior executives, as a go-to source of inspiration and ideas for emerging leaders, or as an essential reference for everyone else. Easy to read, straight to the point, and with depth for almost any workplace situation."

— Richard Dent OAM FAICD, Chief Executive, Leadership Victoria

Dedication

We dedicate this book to our families and loved ones.

Acknowledgements

They say it takes a village to raise a child. We say it takes a community to write a book. We may have typed the words on to the pages but that was just the beginning. Finding the time to work on the book, both as a group and separately, in and around our daily lives, was only made possible by the good graces and unconditional support of our loved ones, to whom we are forever grateful ... again. (Yes, this is our third book together!)

The polishing and refinement of our ever-evolving (and we mean EVER evolving!) ideas and understandings were made possible by our tribe of inspiring, accomplished, wise and supportive mentors. You know who you are and we're sure you know how grateful we are. Just in case you don't – we thank you from the bottom of our hearts for challenging our thinking and calling us forward into our own creativity and contribution.

To our fantastic support team of virtual assistants, editors and designers, we thank you for your patience and professionalism as we waded our way towards to the finish line.

To our clients past and present, we thank you for providing the inspiration (and case studies) for this work. Doing the work we do every day would not be the pleasure it is if it weren't for the calibre of people we get to play with on a daily basis. You have shaped us as experts, you have affected us as people, and you have inspired us to share our experiences beyond our private engagements. It is because of you and your journeys that we are able to share the collective wisdom of growth, learning and the power of potential with the rest of the world. Thank you.

To each of you reading this book, we thank you for investing your time and attention (today's most precious assets), in our work. We thank you for trusting us to provide the value and relevance to make a difference in your world. May this book inform you and inspire you and allow you to connect your people to their potential in new and interesting ways.

A note to the reader

The leadership concepts in this book are explored through the stories of 'Mary' and 'Chris', whose experiences are compilations drawn from our collective client base.

We acknowledge that 'Mary' as the direct report could have easily been 'Mark', and 'Chris' as her manager could have been 'Christine'. We chose to stick with 'Mary' and 'Chris' throughout the book to keep the reading simple and clear.

Table of Contents

About the Authors ....*iii*

Testimonials ....*iv*

Dedication ....*vii*

Acknowledgements ....*ix*

A note to the reader ....*xi*

Introduction 7

How to best use this book 11

Part 1 - Why Develop Your Direct Reports? _____ **17**

Why leadership of leaders needs to change 19

Why developing your direct reports matters 33

Part 2 - How To Develop Your Direct Reports _____ **39**

The mindset for developing leadership performance 41

Three steps to develop your direct reports 53

Leading leaders through a coaching approach 63

Part 3 - The 12 Leadership Derailers _____ **67**

Staller - analysis paralysis 69

Controller - command and control 83

Cyclone - bull at a gate 97

Doer - can't delegate 109

Avoider - conflict averse 125

Fence-sitter - indecisive leader 137

Know-it-all - closed to other ideas 151

Guardian - inability to innovate 163

Micromanager - management on a leash 175

Poker face - showing no emotion 189

People burner - poor people skills 201

Tactician - poor strategic thinker.. 215

Wild Card questions, coaching tips and activities 229

Part 4 - More On The Imperative To Change Leadership Development Right Now _____ **235**

Developing direct reports requires new thinking............................ 237

Performance management is broken 245

Final thoughts... 251

Notes 253

Index.. 261

Introduction

Who should read this book?

Are you ready – ready to connect your direct reports with their leadership potential, and hone your own leadership capacity along the way? This book is for leaders of leaders, who aspire to do better in their roles by developing leadership in others. If you support leadership – people such as coaches, consultants and HR professionals – you too will come away with ideas, practical examples of leadership in action and the wherewithal to truly develop great leadership.

As executive coaches, our role is to help leaders achieve their objectives and potential. The good news is the proof is there. You can learn to develop leadership in others, and lead well. We have witnessed great transformation and we will share the techniques we have used to successfully develop sustainable high performance leadership in this book.

There's a popular saying that suggests, "IQ gets you hired and EQ gets you promoted". We assume that you or your people have the technical expertise needed for the job. However, when technical experts get promoted they don't always have leadership skills; that's where this book will help.

Former Chairman and CEO of General Electric, Jack Welch, said, "Before you are a leader, success is all about growing yourself. When you become a leader, success is all about growing others." We understand how important a leader's leader is to the success of their development. One of the most important roles a leader has is to inspire others to success; so we want to help leaders to do this. This book will help you become a leader who brings out the best in your direct reports. It will improve your understanding of those you lead and will help you to better understand your own behaviour and leadership potential.

A targeted approach

In this book you will learn how to take the guesswork out of developing your direct reports by taking a targeted approach to leadership development. You will understand the value of identifying and responding to the drivers of behaviour, rather than taking a 'one-size-fits-all' approach.

We want to shift leaders from the 'send him/her to a training program' mindset to a targeted and holistic approach to leadership development. Don't get us wrong, we are not anti-training programs (we run them ourselves), but they have limited reach and in this book, we explain why.

We learn best on the job

Targeted development opportunities on the job are where the greatest learning occurs, and feedback must be timely and ongoing. It is all about you fulfilling your role as a developer of people to ensure they reach their potential. This kind of development is more personalised. Through the application of the principles, thinking and techniques shared in this book, you will become confident in having honest development conversations with your direct reports to help them get out of their own way and be greater leaders.

It's all about intention

A Center for Creative Leadership study[1] found that a key factor associated with executive derailment is "having problems with interpersonal relationships". The heart of our work centres on the principle that before you take any action in relation to observed behaviours, you must first understand the positive intentions that drive that behaviour. Like Stephen Covey said, "Seek first to understand and then be understood". It is only when there is true understanding at the next best step can be identified and actioned.

Imagine that you are frustrated that Janine, your recently promoted Operations Manager, is falling further behind and seems to lack basic time management skills. You might be very tempted to send her on a time management course and many leaders do just that. However we know from experience that by the time a person has been promoted to a leadership position, it is unlikely that a skills deficit alone (i.e. time management skills) will be the primary cause of their failure. A different type of approach and conversation is required.

The 12 leadership derailers

As well as providing you with a proven framework for leadership development conversations, this book addresses 12 of the most common leadership derailers in your people. These derailers are the ones we regularly see raised in 360-degree feedback, are often discussed in performance reviews and are frequently addressed inappropriately or not at all.[2]

For each leadership derailer, we provide a framework for targeted behaviour change. This will enable you to address the issue at its root cause rather than applying a band-aid solution that might not be sustained over time. This book won't cover all behaviours, skills and circumstances. There may also be situations that fall outside the scope of this book because they have a deeper psychological base or are just less common. As the saying goes, "If pain persists see your doctor".

We are confident that this book will help you lift the performance of your direct reports. The payback for your efforts will be improved performance of your leaders so they can get the right work done well. We know that when you empower your people to be their best, and do what they love in a way that works, magic happens.

How to best use this book

As individuals, everyone is different and there are endless ways we can filter and apply meaning to the circumstances and events in our lives. Successful leaders are well aware of the challenge this presents. An approach taken with one team member may not be appropriate for another, or even the same person at a later time.

This book offers you the flight path to navigate through common leadership development challenges. We have developed a framework that will assist you to identify and understand the challenge at hand. You'll learn to prepare for and conduct the essential development conversations with your leaders that expand their awareness and equip them to respond.

In selecting the 12 leadership derailers, we referenced both our collective experience as leadership coaches, and the skills the theorists say are essential for today's working environment.[3] We have addressed the areas where we see our clients make the most significant gains for themselves, their team and their organisation.

While not purposely written for you to identify your own development opportunities, we would be surprised if you don't also learn about yourself along the way!

The 12 leadership derailers are:

Staller – analysis paralysis:

From the outside, these leaders are perceived as blockers to progress. They often take too long to take action and therefore risk missing key deadlines or opportunities.

Controller – command and control:

'Control freak' could be another descriptor. These leaders stifle initiative and innovation in their team members as they strive to ensure all goes according to their plan.

Cyclone – bull at a gate:

In a hurry to achieve results, these leaders often leave a wake of destruction (disengaged team members and stakeholders) as they fail to appropriately engage people in their rush to the finish line.

Doer – can't delegate:

Enough said!

Avoider – conflict averse:

Often mistaken for being easygoing or seen as a 'soft touch', these leaders can inadvertently create challenging team dynamics due to their failure to address issues as they arise.

Fence-sitter – indecisive leader:

It is a leader's job to make decisions, every day. Failure to decide equals leadership failure.

Know-it-all – closed to other ideas:

In an age where adaptability is imperative, there is little patience for these leaders who bask in their own brilliance and fail to consider new ideas or input from others. Successful leaders understand that there is always more to learn and knowledge expansion is an everyday sport.

Guardian – inability to innovate:

To stay ahead, companies must continually look for new opportunities. Innovation is the key to business growth and new markets. Leaders who fail to innovate put the role and their organisation at risk.

Micromanager – management on a leash:

A derailer that has been around for as long as we can remember. No one wants to be micromanaged.

Poker face – showing no emotion:

These leaders keep people guessing with their non-expressive communication style. Do they agree? Disagree? Have an opinion? Who knows? While not mincing words, these leaders often fail to apply or see the value of nonverbal communication and often have poor working relationships as a result.

People burner – poor people skills:

These leaders are known for burning people wherever they go to get the job done. For some, it is an unintended consequence; others see achievement of the task as the sole imperative. Whatever the driver, this behaviour is unsustainable.

Tactician – poor strategic thinker:

In our constantly changing global village, thinking ahead to inform the actions of today is paramount. Leaders without this essential skill will stifle their leadership potential and their organisation's success.

As you read through the derailers we are sure you could quickly identify people you know, probably even people in your team. We know that the outward behaviours associated with each derailer are symptomatic of good intentions, poorly executed.

In this book we systematically unpack each derailer. Firstly, we build awareness of the problems associated with each derailer by using a brief scenario to illustrate the commonly seen behaviours and their impacts.

We then consider the underlying positive motivation driving the unresourceful behaviours. We have identified the drivers that we most commonly see, but if it is not one of these, then simply asking: 'What is most important to you in this situation/project/role/your career?' is helpful to elicit the positive intention driving your direct report's poor behaviour.

Once your direct report's intentions are understood then your work commences in earnest. To assist you in establishing a framework for success we have included a snapshot of the latest theory, as well as coaching questions that we regularly use to support behaviour change.

The coaching tips are specific to the derailer under consideration. However, if you are looking for some questions that can be useful irrespective of the context, then check out the Wild Card section towards the back of the book.

As well as providing a specific framework to work through each derailer, we have provided a standard performance discussion framework that will help you to provide targeted coaching in any development conversation. If you are keen to put into practice your 'Leader as Coach' skills, this book will help you hone those skills so you can build your coaching capability while developing others – everybody wins!

Now that you know the high-level approach, it's time to begin.

Part 1

Why Develop Your Direct Reports?

Why leadership of leaders needs to change

The bad news first

Let's start with the bad news: There's no 'user guide' for leading people. There is no one-size-fits-all approach to connecting your leaders with their potential.

Developing people is complex and multifaceted, because people are complex and multifaceted.

Not many leaders we work with complain of being over resourced! Across all sectors leaders are challenged with getting maximum return from their resources, and the people in their team are the most valuable resource. Fit for purpose is important. We need the right people, in the right place, at the right time.

Get to know your people

Maximising your people resource is not straightforward and requires a level of knowledge of human behaviour that many leaders don't yet have. Typically, people are promoted into leadership roles based on their technical skills and expertise, and their leadership capabilities and skills in developing people are not given the same attention.

Neuroscientist Matthew Lieberman, author of *Social: Why Our Brains Are Wired to Connect*, quotes research that found only 0.77 per cent (yes – less than one per cent) of leaders score high on both results focus and strong social skills. He maintains that we are promoting the wrong people, and then giving them insufficient social training when they get there.

"Social skills are a multiplier and allow us to leverage the analytical skills of those around us."[4] So your ability to connect your leaders with their potential will require a conscious focus on developing their social skills.

Rising to the challenge

The good news is that connecting your direct reports with their potential is a skill we can learn. Neuroplasticity is the brain's ability to change—physically, functionally and chemically—throughout life. Neural pathways in the brain are reorganised in response to our experiences and the learning of new skills. This reinforces the possibility that you can build your ability to develop leadership skills in others.

The more challenging question is: what skills do your direct reports need right now?

Over the last 100 years, leadership theorists have spent a great deal of time defining best practice. Leadership theory has evolved from directive, to transformational, to adaptive, and yet there is still no consensus on what makes good leadership, nor how good leadership is developed. This lack of agreement highlights the need for in-time personalised development interventions. The theorists and scientists may never agree and business cannot afford to wait. In the face of this, leaders need to rise to the challenge and develop their people.

About two years ago, Tom Peters felt as if he falling behind. In response, he cleared out his calendar and spent much of the next 18 months reading recent business books. The result? "I'm more confused than when I started," he quips. "My real bottom-line hypothesis is that nobody has a sweet clue what they're doing. Therefore you better be trying stuff at an insanely rapid pace. You want to be screwing around with nearly everything. Relentless experimentation was probably important in the 1970s – now it's do or die."[5]

Developing direct reports

To maximise performance of your team, you need to do more than support the acquisition of additional skills and competencies. To connect leaders with their potential, your role in developing your direct reports is to catalyse increased self-awareness and inspire them to take responsibility for their own leadership development.

Developing direct reports is an aspect of leadership that deals specifically with increasing performance in leaders through targeted conversations that build awareness, motivation and a pathway for action. The conversations are relevant to the individual, robust in nature and conducted in real time.

Sally was a senior executive with decades of experience in operational roles. Previously, she had worked with large teams of people and was considered to be a high performing manager. Sally was then appointed to a strategic role leading a small group of people. After 18 months in the role, Sally sought coaching as she had lost her confidence as a leader. Her manager had told her that her team had complained about her leadership style and failure to engage them in the work of the group. Sally identified that her preference for fast-paced action and outcomes in the here and now, which was ideal for her former roles, was proving inappropriate in the strategic space and derailing her leadership. By properly identifying the heart of her leadership challenge she was able to redirect her focus through targeted action.

For sustained change, your leaders will be best served by making small incremental changes that target specific behaviours. In our experience, small targeted changes can make a big difference to performance.

Five reasons why developing direct reports is essential for you now

1. WORKPLACES HAVE CHANGED

In a relatively short period historically, the work that we do and the way that we do it, has changed significantly. Over the last 100 years we have replaced our bodies, and later, even parts of our minds with machines. Our workplaces have evolved from farms, to factories, to Facebook.[6]

In the past, there was an unwritten psychological contract between employers and employees that loyal and hardworking employees would be granted a 'job for life'.[7] Today, career development means multiple employers within a person's career[8] with employees looking for companies that provide professional development, career growth, job challenge, flexibility and a strong employment brand.[9]

CARROTS NO LONGER WORK

Managing people applying the 'carrot and stick' approach doesn't drive performance outside the factory. The psychological contract has changed and now companies must engage their employees. Unfortunately, achieving employee engagement is not straight-forward. We agree that a positive emotional attachment to the work and organisation is central to effective employee engagement. However 'engagement' means different things to different people. This makes engagement a moving target for organisations seeking to improve their performance.[10]

ENGAGED EMPLOYEES PUT MORE EFFORT IN

The value of employee engagement is the discretionary effort that comes with it. This effort leads employees to go above and beyond in their work just because they can and it makes them feel good. If this can be harnessed (and these efforts are aligned with organisational objectives), then magic happens. Performance increases by 20 per cent, as does business performance and shareholder returns[11] and costly attrition is reduced.[12]

Unfortunately, research indicates that more than 70 per cent of the workforce at most companies is not fully engaged. This presents a significant challenge for leaders.[13] Optimum performance will never be achieved on the strength of technical expertise alone. To achieve organisational objectives and fulfil their roles and career potential, they must also develop leadership skills that are influential in identifying and harnessing the intrinsic motivation of those that they lead. If you have spent most of your life training in a technical speciality, the step up into a leadership role can often feel like starting out all over again.

2. ADAPTABILITY IS NOT NEGOTIABLE

This change in the way we work is characterised by the need to work faster and apply advanced thinking capabilities to stay ahead in a rapidly changing environment. It is no longer about 'what you know' and 'who you know'. Outstanding leaders need to know what needs to change, and they need to adapt quickly to stay relevant.

WE COMPETE GLOBALLY – LIKE IT OR NOT

Organisations now compete in a fast-changing global environment. Globalisation has led to economies being more closely linked than ever before. In a boom there is global prosperity. However a chink in the world's economic armour can lead to a global financial crisis, as was experienced in 2008. Economically, we are like the occupants of a snow globe where even the smallest shake can have far reaching effects for many.

An IBM study of over 1500 CEOs projects an image of our future working environment being in a perpetual state of chaos.[14] Many CEOs involved in the study used the army acronym VUCA[15] to describe the new environment:

- **Volatile:** change happens rapidly and on a large scale.

- **Uncertain:** the future cannot be predicted with any precision.

- **Complex:** challenges are complicated by many factors and there are few single causes or solutions.

- **Ambiguous:** there is little clarity on what events mean and what effect they may have.

YOU NEED YOUR 'A' GAME DAILY

With many unknowns and much new territory to navigate, there is more pressure than ever on leaders today to bring their 'A' game. Organisations are actively competing to attract and retain the best leaders. Unfortunately, research shows "a significant gap between the urgency of the talent and the leadership issues leaders face today, and their organisation's readiness to respond."[16]

But how do you define 'the best' when it comes to leadership in a VUCA environment? What are the ideal leadership qualities?

3. TODAY'S LEADER IS NOT TOMORROW'S LEADER

The heroic individual leader has been the gold standard for leadership over the last 40 years and, consequently, leadership theorists have developed endless models in an attempt to define the characteristics and qualities of the 'ideal leader'. However, even though leadership studies have been prolific over the last 100 years, no conclusive framework has been agreed. As leadership coaches, we are not surprised by this. When we work with clients, as well as their individual objectives, it's also critical to consider the environment and specific context in which they operate. Good leadership in one context may not be good leadership in another.

Jeffrey was a gifted project manager with a strong reputation across his industry for bringing projects in within time and budget. Preferring the variety of contract work, he was often brought in at the last minute when a project was going off the rails. IT executives knew Jeffrey would deliver and were willing to pay handsomely for his services. And deliver he always did.

After years of moving in and out of organisations, Jeffrey was ready for a change of pace, and joined a community-based organisation in a leadership role. He wanted to develop longer-term relationships and also to 'give back' to the community. The organisation wanted his project leadership skills and delivery focus as they introduced a project focus to their way of operation.

After six weeks, Jeffrey's team was ready to mutiny and key stakeholders were refusing to work with him. It was clear that the style that had served Jeffrey well for many years in the IT&T space was not successful in the community sector.

MANY FACTORS

Leadership is also not solely a function of hierarchy or location. Companies now have access to a global talent market and a fast-developing mobile global workforce.[17] Consequently, this increasingly complex work environment is less suited to problem solving by a lone, decisive authority figure. It requires the collaborative efforts of a network of smart, flexible leaders who may work at varying levels within an organisation. Working together to share knowledge, this network of leaders understands that the 'whole is greater than the sum of its parts' but, that equally, each part has an essential role to play.

The study of leadership theory[18] is ongoing and will continue to attempt to provide a narrative, evidence and guidance for the leaders of tomorrow. In our view, our change-driven global working environment means that is unlikely that a one-size-fits-all definition can be achieved and nor should it be.

It makes sense that the theory and practices that have supported us in the past and present, may not work in the future. The rules of the game have changed and will continue to do so.

4. LEARNING AGILITY IS ESSENTIAL

Leadership in any organisation should support the achievement of the organisation's immediate and future objectives; consequently leaders need to be continually evolving their skills. A 2014 global study by Deloitte (which included more than 2,500 businesses across 94 countries), found that leadership remains the number one talent issue facing organisations globally, with 86 per cent of respondents rating it as 'urgent' or 'important'. This finding was also consistent across all industries. Unfortunately, the study also found that companies showed low levels of readiness to respond with a notable capability shortfall in leadership.[19]

CONSTANT CHANGE REQUIRES LEARNING AGILITY

This urgent need for leadership is driven by globalisation and the speed and expanse of technological change, which creates high levels of uncertainty. In an environment of change learning agility is paramount. Leaders must be adaptable and willing to let go of the 'old ways'. They need to learn new approaches as they climb up the career ladder.[20]

REHASHING THE PAST DOESN'T WORK

Many leaders derail because they remain focused on the skills and competencies that got them promoted, and they stop learning the skills they need to be an effective leader.[21] Canvassing just the last 10 years, leaders will have had to unlearn methodologies, technologies, ways of communicating, client relationship management strategies and outdated leadership styles, just to name a few. This can be easier said than done.

Both leaders and their team members must be learning agile.[22] To get the best out of their team, leaders need to proactively support and develop their people (and themselves) to be the leaders that their people, organisation and industry need. A leader must continually learn and grow, taking the time to reflect on what worked and what didn't. This largely occurs on the job and requires them to take the learning from one situation and apply it to a different context.[23] It is an ongoing process of discovery and application.

Your success is going to be made or broken on the strength of the leaders you lead. While technology might be the foundation for a business, it is the actions of the people who run the business that determines whether it succeeds or fails. By investing in those that you lead you are investing in the future growth of yourself and your organisation.

5. LEADERSHIP IS LEARNABLE

In the past, leaders who behaved badly were tolerated. The boss knew it all and no one expected him to change. There is no room for this excuse anymore. Numerous scientific studies undertaken since the 1970s have established that the brain has the capacity to re-wire itself and change its structure and function well into old age. Departing from the centuries-old view that the adult brain is static and unchanging, the concept of neuroplasticity has changed our perspective on how we view the brain. More importantly, it has enhanced our understanding of our ability to actively influence our human potential through active management of our thinking and behaviour.[24]

LEARNING EFFORT IS REWARDED

Changing the brain's structure involves creating new, or strengthening existing, neural connections and weakening/eliminating others; learning, unlearning and relearning. More significant learning interventions require more profound neural modification, which for you means more effort for longer. As Nobel Prize winner and author, Daniel Kahneman, has said, "True intuitive expertise is learned from prolonged experience with good feedback on mistakes."

IF YOU'RE MOTIVATED, YOU CAN DO IT

We are excited by the findings as they provide the scientific explanation for the behavioural changes we have observed in our clients. The ability to influence the wiring of our brain creates inspiring possibilities for expanding performance potential. Ranging from improved cognition and perception through to acquiring new skills and enhanced behavioural flexibility. We have observed that with awareness, motivation and supported action, shifts in individual performance are achievable and sustainable.

So you may be thinking ...

"I don't have time for all this!" Our challenge to you is that you don't have time to not do it! The cost of your leader(s) not performing is absorbing time you don't have.

There's no need to read this book cover to cover. If you have a direct report with an obvious derailer you may wish to leap straight into the relevant chapter so you can focus quickly on their immediate leadership development needs.

While we provide the framework, it's up to you to develop your direct report. While knowing is good, it's doing that generates results!

"What's the theory behind this?" This is not an academic approach to leadership. We focus on results. While we refer to some of the latest leadership thinking, our key value comes from translating theoretical concepts into real world results. Results informed by our years of experience developing leaders, and shared in this practical how-to guide.

"I am not a coach so I can't do this." Just as a beginner can create fabulous art through colouring by numbers, we are confident you will be able to follow this step-by-step guide.

"Is this just focusing on the problems and ignoring the strengths?" As coaches we start with and focus on core strengths. We are also aware of derailers that can result in core strengths being undermined, overlooked or even overused. Think about a high performance car driven by someone who has unknowingly left the handbrake on. Until the brake is released, the car won't go fast no matter how hard the pedal is pushed, and the engine could be damaged in the meantime.

You picked up this book because 'developing direct reports' resonated with you. You may have also been thinking some of these thoughts above, and now it's up to you to make a decision. How important is developing direct reports to you? To your team? Your organisation? It's time to decide and take action.

SUMMARY

- Developing people is complex. There is no one-size-fits-all approach.
- Neuroscience confirms leadership can be learned.
- Leaders need to act as the catalyst and coach to connect their leaders to their potential.
- Small, targeted development changes can make a big difference to performance.
- The carrot and stick approach no longer works outside the factory. Engagement is the answer.
- Adaptability is the essential skill in the 21st century workplace. Leaders need to adapt for optimum role and organisational fit.
- The heroic standalone leader has been replaced with a network of leaders.
- Leadership is learnable and this will include learning, unlearning and relearning.

Why developing your direct reports matters

If a fundamental role of the leader is to develop their direct reports and connect them with their potential, how well are you doing?

The Performance Development Ladder

	direct report	LEADER	productivity
Increasing return	amplified	INSPIRATIONAL	x6
	active	INSIGHTFUL	x4
	awakening	INQUISITIVE	x2
	ambivalent	INCONSISTENT	x1
Increasing cost	absent	INDIFFERENT	x -2

Indifferent

At the bottom of the Performance Development Ladder, the **Indifferent** leader pays little attention to their direct report. We are confident this isn't you because an indifferent leader would never dedicate time and energy to reading a book like this. When you don't actively support your direct reports to develop, you might find them **Absent**. This absence may be reflected in their attitude, commitment, output and focus, as well as actual absenteeism. Perhaps even worse for them and the organisation, they might not actually leave. Being absent can have a destructive impact on the direct reports themself, on the team culture and on you.

According to the Dale Carnegie Institute, "… it is the immediate supervisor who is the chief emotional driver in the workplace; reactions to him or her explain 84% of how employees feel about their organization."[25]

Inconsistent

Perhaps you are **Inconsistent** in your efforts to develop your direct reports, or you struggle to know how to help some of them, leaving them professionally *Ambivalent*. They are not motivated to leave but don't feel they are developing. This level of ineffectiveness is a lost opportunity for you and the organisation.

John was in the inconsistent space. He intended to support and develop his people and, being very task focussed, he found himself focussing on outcomes at the expense of people. Aware that this was happening, he would consciously shift his attention to the needs of his people for a few days, usually prompted by the twice-yearly performance review cycle, and then his attention would return to the tasks at hand. Having a confrontation with the CEO about the high turnover in John's divisional leadership team was the trigger for him to seek the help of a coach.

Inquisitive

Moving up the ladder, at **Inquisitive** you are *Awakening*, learning and creating capable leaders. Yet there is still significant untapped potential.

Adam is an engineer who describes himself as a 'people person'. He is inquisitive about, and supportive of, what drives people, and is concerned for their welfare. Yet despite his natural people focus, he lacks the people development skills to capitalise on their potential.

There is a tipping point here, where you can really see increasing return on your investment in your direct report.

The **Insightful** leader creates *Aware* leaders who are able to effectively lead themselves and their teams. Here, your people are aware of their behaviours and their impact. They are aware of potential disconnects between their inside intention and outside behaviour, and are skilled and empowered to take targeted action.

Amelia leads a large division of a major public hospital. Working with her leaders, she provides regular feedback that creates awareness in her team. Her special gift is providing feedback that both connects to the organisational purpose, and leaves the leader empowered to respond. This hasn't happened by magic; Amelia has worked hard to understand herself and her own drivers, and remain true to her values as a leader despite the significant leadership challenges she has faced.

Inspirational

At the top of the Performance Development Ladder is **Inspirational**. You inspire your direct reports to be more than they see themselves capable of being. Your leadership **amplifies** their capabilities, empowering them to fully realise their potential while leveraging the full potential of their team.

Barry is described by staff, clients and stakeholders alike as inspirational. He has built a social welfare company from $0 to $40m over 25 years, creating an inspired and inspiring organisation that has significantly influenced the Australian policy landscape. He has been able to do that through developing his direct reports and creating a strong executive leadership team that operates both autonomously and interdependently. Barry's special skill is to raise everyone's performance to greater heights than they thought possible.

SUMMARY

- The Performance Development Ladder helps leaders know how well they are developing their direct reports.

- An Indifferent leader creates an absent direct report and negatively impacts productivity.

- An Inconsistent leader creates an ambivalent direct report and does not make a positive impact on productivity.

- An Inquisitive leader creates an awakening direct report and can double the productivity of the direct report.

- An Insightful leader creates an active direct report and can more than double the productivity of the direct report.

- An Inspirational leader creates an amplified direct report and can significantly impact the productivity capacity of the direct report.

- The higher up the ladder the leader is in terms of their style for developing direct reports, the more they increase their impact on the direct report from a place of diminishing returns to a place of increasing returns.

Part 2

How To Develop Your Direct Reports

The mindset for developing leadership performance

A coaching approach is what you will need for effective leadership development discussions. Research undertaken by Bersin & Associates[26] found that organisations in which senior leaders were frequently coached had 21 per cent higher business results. Here is the mindset that underpins a coaching approach for developing your direct reports.

Ten key principles for developing your direct reports (your mindset matters)

1. NO ONE IS BROKEN

There is no wrong or right, good or bad. This is simply about what works. Our frame for development is non-judgmental. It is never about making an individual wrong or finding fault, but rather examining the circumstances at hand and determining what worked and what didn't. We regularly see clients who demonstrate a set of behaviours in one environment with an acceptable response, and then behave the same way in a different environment and receive adverse feedback. When this occurs, the client has simply failed to adapt their behaviour to suit the context.

Anthony was the MD of a privately listed company. Early in his career, he was well known and respected for his ability to jump on new ideas and initiatives. As he developed into more senior roles though, his tendency to jump into new initiatives over and over again, created major ripples of anxiety and irritation through the rest of the company. Employees complained that there was never enough time to deliver anything. Before they had begun to implement the first idea the next

*one was already on its way and they had to change course again.
The pace of change brought about by the MD was too high for
the rest of the business to effectively execute any good ideas and
resulted in frustration and a lack of engagement across the business.
So Anthony's focus on constantly seeking innovation and new ideas
supported him to do well in his early career, but in his senior roles it
worked against him.*

2. LOOK FOR THE POSITIVE INTENTION

Separating observable behaviours from the intentions that drive them
provides insight and greater scope to influence and develop your direct
report. Behaviour that seems unproductive on the surface, regardless of
how it looks, largely comes from a positive intention. Your challenge is
to hold that belief when faced with undesirable behaviours in your direct
report. When working to develop others and deconstructing behaviours,
it is imperative that the intention is identified, as this opens the door to
exploring alternative pathways for achieving the same end.

PERCEPTIONS DON'T HELP

The important thing to remember is that a person's behaviours and
actions depend on their subjective perception, which may in that
moment be adversely influenced by cognitive bias. One example of a
cognitive bias is the fundamental attribution error[27], also known as the
attribution effect. This is the tendency to place an undue emphasis on
internal characteristics to explain someone else's behaviour rather than
considering external factors.

As a simple example, consider a situation where Amanda is disappointed
with an event organiser because she has failed to provide Amanda with
a quotation within the requested deadline. The fundamental attribution
error may lead Amanda to think that the event organiser is incompetent
and doesn't care about the business. This will be an error if the event
organiser had a good reason for failing to respond, such as not receiving

Amanda's email requesting the quotation. If this is the case and Amanda had known this, she would have understood the reason why there was no response and taken follow-up action rather than judging the behaviour as an indication of a personality flaw.

LOOK FOR THE TRUE MOTIVATION

When the fundamental attribution error is removed, a person's true motivation is revealed. Revealing the positive intention is a central premise as it enables you to perceive your direct report in a completely different light, and coach and develop them more effectively.

When you separate the behaviours from the intentions, judgment falls away. More importantly, negative perceptions are replaced with curiosity, which leads to understanding and insight for both the leader and the direct report.

3. WHAT YOU EXPECT IS WHAT YOU GET – PYGMALION EFFECT

The Pygmalion effect[28] is a psychological principal that describes people's propensity to live up to the high expectations you hold of them. When translated to leadership this can create a form of self-fulfilling prophecy for those that we lead. When we expect a leader to rise to the challenge of a new role, and we support them to do so, they will.

THE OPPOSITE IS ALSO TRUE

Contrast this with the Golem effect, producing the same but opposite effect; people perform poorly when expected to. For example, if a leader expects an employee to fail at a given task then there is a high likelihood that they will.

The upshot for you? You get what you expect when it comes to developing performance in others. What you hold possible for your direct report sets the frame that they can grow into. Your expectations can serve to either lift them or limit them. Be clear on the judgments, expectations and beliefs you hold about your direct report. Expect and encourage the best from the leaders you are developing.

Ideas for when you don't like your direct report
- **Watch** *how your direct report positively interacts and engages with others. Focus on observable positive behaviours and key strengths.*
- **Listen** *to understand what motivates them, what are their goals/ problems and how do they view you, their team members and their work? How does their perspective provide unique and valuable insight not offered by others in the team?*
- **Experiment** *to change how you react to challenging behaviours. Rather than responding quickly in the moment, take a breath. Regroup and redirect by eliciting the positive intention.*
- **Meet** *regularly to learn more. Connection builds understanding.*
- **Reach out** *to know what your direct reports do outside the office. Watch and listen to how skilled, motivated and interesting they can be.*

---

4. IT'S OKAY TO NOT HAVE ALL THE ANSWERS

People are complex and there will always be some behaviours you do not understand. When supporting your direct report, your role is to support the exploration. Resist offering solutions and filling the silence.

LET THEM EVOLVE TO THE ANSWER

From a physiological perspective it is important that your direct report comes to their own answers. David Rock in his book, *Quiet Leadership: Six Steps to Transforming Performance at Work*[29], details his findings into what he describes as "the anatomy of an 'aha' [moment]". He describes a four-stage process to reach the new insight. First, the coachee presents with a dilemma, then they reflect internally. This gives off alpha-band waves that trigger the release of serotonin and helps them to feel good about the process of reflecting. Then, the moment of insight occurs. This causes a rush of energy driven both by the new set of connections being developed in the brain (a new view of the world/ or the dilemma), and by adrenalin and other brain chemicals such as serotonin and dopamine. Given that fear can often be the reason why a coachee has not made the change until this point in time, this rush of energy is critical to helping a direct report to push through and take action anyway. With this rush of energy, the coachee is moved into the motivation phase and is more likely to take action. However, this rush of energy does not last long. So it is imperative that the coachee takes tangible actions as soon as possible, or at the very least commit to doing something later that will trigger the new reality.

What does that mean for advice? Our response would be, where possible don't give it. The delivering of a packaged solution can prevent the coachee from experiencing the energetic rush they need to motivate themselves into action. At the very least, if you want to provide your own insight, make sure this is presented as ideas or alternatives for their consideration, and then leave the rest to them.

5. THE DIRECT REPORT IS RESPONSIBLE

Sustained change requires sustained effort and the responsibility for making the change stays with them. There will be effort on your part to support your direct report, however your efforts should not exceed their efforts. Your job is to hold your direct report accountable for their development. Do not be emotionally blackmailed into thinking that you are responsible. Be clear how you can support them and commit to doing that. The rest is up to them.

6. LISTEN AND LISTEN SOME MORE

Listening is critical to developing your direct report. Sometimes allowing the person to be heard is all that is needed to begin the development journey. When we coach we listen for what is not said; for global statements applied to numerous contexts; for closed thinking; for strong beliefs and the positive intention. The most effective way for you to listen to all of these things is to say nothing while demonstrating your authentic commitment to understanding and supporting your direct report.

7. CONSCIOUS USE OF QUESTIONS

Questions are an art form, and articulate, open questions have the potential to unleash insightful conversations. A closed question has a 'yes' or 'no' answer, and doesn't involve the brain in a creative search for answers. An open question that requires more than a one-word answer opens up possibilities.

To steer your questions wisely, use open questions at the beginning of the conversation to open up thinking. Use closed questions towards the end of a performance conversation to narrow down possibilities and support decision-making.

8. REINFORCE POSITIVE BEHAVIOUR

When we want to encourage a particular behaviour, we need to identify and reward that. In their book *Switch*, Chip and Dan Heath talk about 'approximations'.[30] Animal trainers set a behavioural destination, and then reward approximations; tiny steps on the way to the desired behaviour. Think of training Fido. He won't 'sit' the first time you tell him to. You give him little doggy treats along the way each time he gets closer to 'sit'.

Criticism is too easy. To encourage behavioural change this must stop. As a leader you must notice and encourage small approximations of the behaviour you want. Reinforcement is essential as your direct report takes the necessary steps on their longer journey of change.

9. GET YOUR DIRECT REPORT TO DECIDE

The decision to act is the first step on any journey. Research from the Center for Creative Leadership shows that people develop faster when they take responsibility for their own development.[31] If they do decide for themselves, this triggers their core motivational drivers, tapping into the inherent urge to get better and achieve our own level of mastery.[32]

10. ROME WASN'T BUILT IN A DAY

At an individual neuron level our brains are built to detect environmental changes and alert us to anything unusual or out of the ordinary. These 'error detection signals' are sent from the emotional centre of the brain, which directly competes with our rational brain for resources. When these error detection signals are sent out, our emotional brain takes over. Given the brain science, it is therefore understandable why change triggers fear and anxiety.

When a decision to change is made, this redirects our attention to something new. This focus on something new leads to new neural connections and physical changes in the brain. The more opportunities the brain has to be exposed to this new focus through stimulating environments and directed activities, the more connections that are made, leading to improved performance. This process is known as self-directed neuroplasticity.[33]

As the process suggests, repetition is the key. Discrete goals and repeated efforts are required. For you as a leader, this means that you must continually support your direct report as they go through this process to create the desired brain change.

Four fundamental mindsets
(the direct report's focus matters too)

Now you are clear on the mindset required to develop your direct reports, what about them?

Here is the fundamental thinking that will support your direct report in their development.

1. COMMITTED TO CHANGE

The premise of this book is supporting behaviour change, and there is an assumption that your direct report wants to change. In a study published by the Center for Creative Leadership[34], "inability or unwillingness to change or adapt" was found to be a key factor associated with leadership derailment across cultures.

For change to occur, even with your support, it is fundamental that the direct report makes a decision or commitment to change. It is only then that your work together can begin.

2. OPEN TO NEW IDEAS AND APPROACHES

For the direct report to develop new leadership capabilities, they must be open to new ideas and approaches. If they continue to do what they have always done they will continue to get the same results.

3. READY TO TAKE ACTION

All change starts with awareness, but knowing is not doing. The key is moving from insight to action.

4. WILLING TO SOLICIT AND RECEIVE FEEDBACK

Consistent with the learning, unlearning, relearning principle, successful behaviour change requires a cycle of continued feedback to refine and improve performance.

Five other factors that may impact success

In addition to the mindsets needed for successful leadership development, there are other factors to be aware of that may influence a successful development outcome.

1) SELF-IDENTITY

People can believe, "this is just the way I am. I can't change". They have mistakenly made their behaviours part of their fixed identity, so change seems harder. The leadership derailers in this book are behaviourally based and therefore can be shifted. Have a conversation about the changeable brain so they understand and believe that change is possible for them.

2) ORGANISATIONAL CULTURE

Organisational culture is a powerful influence on leadership style. This includes both the formal organisational culture and the 'shadow system', or informal culture, which shapes the organisational dynamic. The CEO of one financial services organisation we worked with was keen to develop innovation in his leadership team. Recently arrived from a dynamic organisation, he was surprised to find his team resistant to trialling new ideas. It soon became clear that in the recent organisational history there was a major public relations disaster after a miscalculated risk had backfired, and now both the board and executive were highly risk averse. The company's values statement included 'innovation' and yet the shadow culture was counter to fostering innovation.

3) EXTERNAL ENVIRONMENT

External environmental context is also relevant. For example, a leader attempting to inspire the development of collaboration in their direct report within a highly competitive and declining market sector, would need to be conscious of the external environmental push back reinforcing competition over collaboration.

4) INTERNAL ENVIRONMENTAL

Internal environmental context can provide an additional overlay of complexity. For example, the risk appetite of an organisation may be low and yet your direct report is being asked to take more risk.

5) YOUR LEADERSHIP STYLE

Your leadership style and beliefs, as we saw in the 10 mindset principles above, will influence your direct report's success.

SUMMARY

- A coaching approach is needed for effective leadership development discussions.
- The mindset of the leader is what supports a coaching approach to developing others.
- The ten mindset principles for developing direct reports include:
    - No one is broken
    - Look for the positive intention behind the behaviour
    - What you expect is what you get – Pygmalion effect
    - It's okay to not have all the answers
    - The direct report is responsible
    - Listen and listen some more
    - Conscious use of questions
    - Reinforce positive behaviour
    - Get your direct report to decide
    - Rome wasn't built in a day

- The four fundamental mindsets of the direct report include:
  - Committed to change
  - Open to new ideas and approaches
  - Ready to take action
  - Willing to solicit and receive feedback
- The other factors that also impact success include:
  - Self-identity
  - Organisational culture
  - External environment
  - Internal environment
  - Your leadership style

Three steps to develop your direct reports

Here is the 3D Development Model for developing your direct reports. The three key elements are:

- **Discover** – Build awareness of the need for change.
- **Decode** – Create insight and understanding of the underlying drivers causing the behaviour.
- **Design** – Agree on the pathway and actions required to create new behaviours.

The **context** for change is also critical. The environment in which development is undertaken will influence both the approach and the outcome. Only by understanding the context that all parties and the organisation are working within, can the leader put truth around the three elements.

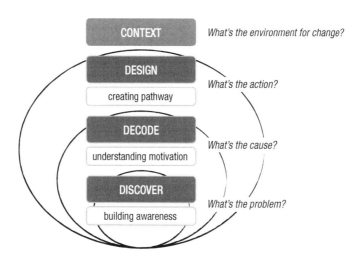

Discover – what's the problem?

Deciding which leadership behaviours to develop in your direct reports requires them to have awareness of their behaviours and the resulting impacts for themselves and others. Awareness is important because it precedes change, it directs change and it creates motivation. Let's take a closer look at the importance of developing awareness in your direct reports.

THE LIGHT BULB HAS TO WANT TO CHANGE

Awareness precedes change. 'Awareness is 95 per cent of the journey' is a maxim often used in coaching. People can't change what they are not aware of and yet creating awareness of behaviours to change can be a big step. Research suggests that people are not good judges of their own behavioural competencies.[35] With numerous biases clouding our perceptions[36], it can be hard for your direct report to see themselves objectively, or to know what needs to change.

Awareness directs change. It is not enough to know that 'something' needs to change. Direct reports must know the specific behaviours that they want to change in order for them to direct their focus. The greater their ability to pinpoint exactly what's working, what's not working and why, the greater their ability to develop the desired leadership behaviours.

AWARENESS CREATES MOTIVATION

Awareness contributes to the motivation necessary to sustain the effort to make a sustainable change. Creating new behaviours takes time and in order to stay the course, people need to be intrinsically motivated; they need to care. They also need to know where they are heading, why it's important and what's at stake if they don't get there.

DISCOVERING THE PROBLEM BY BUILDING SELF-AWARENESS IN YOUR DIRECT REPORT

Here are five key ways to build your direct report's self-awareness:

1. Questioning to expand their perspective

2. Reflecting back observations

3. Giving direct feedback

4. Providing new information (articles, blogs, books, courses, etc.)

5. Encouraging self-reflection

Each of the 12 performance derailers includes a framework for presenting direct feedback, as well as questions to encourage self-reflection and build awareness.

Using a combination of the five awareness builders will provide more than enough insight for your direct report to discover what's really going on and decide on the changes they want to make.

Give me the bad news!

People want to hear the full story of their performance ... warts and all. They want the constructive feedback as much as the positive feedback. Unfortunately leaders don't want to give constructive feedback as much as their direct reports want to hear it.[37]

1 Don't hold back on critical feedback. You are doing your direct report a disservice by not allowing them to become aware of what they can do to develop.

2 Get good at giving critical feedback (skilfully)! Your people want to hear it but they still need to be able to swallow it.

BUILDING YOUR SELF-AWARENESS

Your level of awareness is also crucial to your direct report's development journey. You need to be aware of how your own judgments, beliefs and biases can impact their ability to develop under your leadership.

Here are our top three tips for building your own self-awareness.

1. **Check yourself before challenging them.**
    Sometimes behaviours in others are magnified or minimised only when compared to our own. For example, if you have a tendency to make very quick decisions, then you may judge others who make decisions more slowly than you to be 'very slow to decide'. In fact, they may be quite normal when it comes to the speed of decision-making, but when you compare them to yourself (being much faster than average), they can appear slow. Before judging the behaviours of your direct report be sure to know how your own behaviours stack up.

2. **Adhere to the essential mindset.**
    Put into action what you have read.

3. **Get coached.**
    To fast-track your self-awareness, get coached. Get a buddy, a boss or a professional to work with you and provide an independent perspective. Remember that we can't see ourselves as clearly as others. So reach out, get feedback, get perspective or even use this book on yourself first!

BEFORE DIVING IN

Here are five questions to ask yourself prior to taking your direct report on this journey of discovery:

*   What are you doing right now to build the awareness of your direct report?

*   Where is there room for improvement?

- How are your expectations of your direct report impacting their development?
- What beliefs do you have about their capacity to change and develop?
- How might some of your own behaviours be impacting their leadership development?

Decode – what's the cause?

Trying to change behaviours without addressing the underlying motivational drivers is like painting the car red and expecting it to go faster. Changing the paint colour does not change the engine.

All behaviour is motivated. People are driven by conscious and unconscious drivers. These can include: the environment, capabilities, beliefs, values, identity, memories, past experiences, upbringing, culture, etc. There will be motivators driving the behaviour of your direct report that you are not aware of. Your direct report may not even be consciously aware of them either.

LET THEM DISCOVER THEIR MOTIVATORS

You don't necessarily need to know the underlying drivers of your direct report's behaviour. Your job is to facilitate a dialogue with them to discover their own motivational drivers. They will then be able to harness their energy and redirect their behaviour in a way that better supports their intention. This is like lifting the bonnet of the car to help them understand how their engine works.

You may gain insights into some common unconscious motivational drivers for the behaviour concerned by reading the specific performance derailers. These can provide a starting point for a conversation. The coaching questions and tips are designed specifically to support your direct report to uncover their own 'aha' moments.

Design – what's the action?

Once your direct report is clear on what they want to develop, you need to help them design their pathway for improved performance.

You play a vital role in supporting them to design a plan that is actionable, realistic and relevant (to them and their career as well as the business). You may have information about the business objectives that they don't have, and so will need to guide their plan.

Once the plan is in place it's about supporting them to stay the course.

How? Through ongoing conversations about what they are doing, how it is going, what needs to change and what they need from you. (Refer to development conversations framework on pg. 63)

Behaviour change is created by taking focused action over time. Knowing is not enough. Doing translates insight to action. When the doing is done on the job, new behaviours are integrated faster and more completely.

The brain needs time

New habits and behaviours are created when the brain has time to build new neural pathways that support the new thinking and action. These new pathways are cemented through focused attention and repetition of new choices over time. As their leader you can make or break their ability to build these new skills. Your direct report needs job-relevant assignments where they can practise their new ways of behaving. They need permission to fail and feedback to refine their behaviour and integrate the learning. Most importantly, they need to know that you've got their back along the way.

When it comes to taking action to develop and enact the plan, support them by:

- bringing your knowledge of the greater business context and organisational goals into the discussion to align their leadership development with business objectives

- helping them to practise their new behaviours as much as possible and provide feedback to help them grow

- remembering that behaviour change takes time and be prepared to support them through the ups and downs while the new behaviours integrate.

Context – understanding the environment for change

Context is critical because context creates the frame through which the development is shaped. The context can be anything in the immediate environment that can potentially influence the success of your direct report's leadership development. This includes influences like the organisation and team culture, leadership style and trust levels, as well as the political, social, technological and environmental landscape.

The context can be a driving factor for the behaviours that need to be developed, and that impact success. A behaviour that may drive high performance in one environment may jeopardise performance in another. Windscreen wipers are ineffective in the sunshine but in the rain their value is undeniable.

Along with the *discovery* of what needs to change, the *decoding* of the motivational drivers and *designing* a clear pathway to enact the change, the *context* is the final element of the 3D Development Model. Together, these components provide the framework for developing your direct reports.

SUMMARY

- The three steps to creating behaviour change are: discover, decode and design the pathway.

- Discover the problem: use questions to expand their perspective; reflect back their observations; give direct feedback; deliver new information and encourage self-reflection.

- Build your own awareness: think before speaking; put the 3D Development Model into action for yourself and get coaching.

- Decode motivation: Understand that all behaviour is motivated; help your direct report discover their own motivation.

- Design the pathway: Create a flexible, personalised action plan.

- Allocate time for the development conversation to happen.

- Know the context you are encouraging your direct report within; this is critical.

Leading leaders through a coaching approach

We recommend supporting the leadership development of your direct reports through a coaching approach. Regular conversations about your direct report's progress allows them to drive their own development process.

There are many ways to have this conversation and to get you started we have codified and simplified what works for us as leadership coaches.

Development conversation framework

As you conduct these conversations, remember that embodying the mindsets outlined earlier will assist you to set the tone that will create a safe and constructive environment for you and your direct report.

PREPARATION

1. Review your organisation's or department's long-term goals (one to three years). This builds context and allows you to easily align your direct report's actions with the goals of the organisation.

2. Review the role your direct report actually does and be clear on what you want them to be doing. Don't just rely on what their job description document says. In our experience this is often an outdated and/or ignored source document.

3. Get clear on your direct report's key focus for the next 90 days.

4. Understand and be prepared to explain if needed, how their key focus aligns to the key business drivers.

5. Review the list of derailers to build your perspective on what you think your direct report needs to work on.

CONVERSATION

6. **Discover – what's the problem?** Meet with your direct report to explore and build awareness on the most important derailers to address their development needs.

7. **Decode – what's the cause?** Use the derailer description to facilitate a discussion around possible intentions that are driving the behaviours, and understand underlying motivations.

8. **Design – what's the action?** Create a pathway forwards – develop a targeted plan from the Coaching Tips (and Wild Cards if needed) to shift the identified behaviours that drive the derailer.
a) Be ready to suggest business activities, tasks or projects where your direct report can apply their new behaviours and get supportive feedback.
b) Agree on the support needed to develop these behaviours. You may include introductions to new people to shadow and learn from, accountability checks, resources and references like books, journals, videos, as well as how much feedback is required, etc.
c) Agree on an accountability framework so you are both clear on your roles and how often to follow up on progress, including timeframes for regular check-ins between you and your direct report.

FOLLOW-UP

9. Ensure you follow up with your direct report as agreed in the performance conversation.

10. Provide regular constructive and specific feedback.

11. Encourage and celebrate successes, both small and large.

In order to use this framework above we have assumed you already have a working knowledge of 'leader as coach' concepts. If a coaching style is unfamiliar to you, we strongly recommend a development program to build these skills.

SUMMARY

- Regular coaching conversations about your direct report's progress allows them to drive their own development process.
- The Development conversation framework consists of three parts: Preparation, Conversation and Follow-up.
- Follow the Development conversation framework to create safe and constructive conversations.

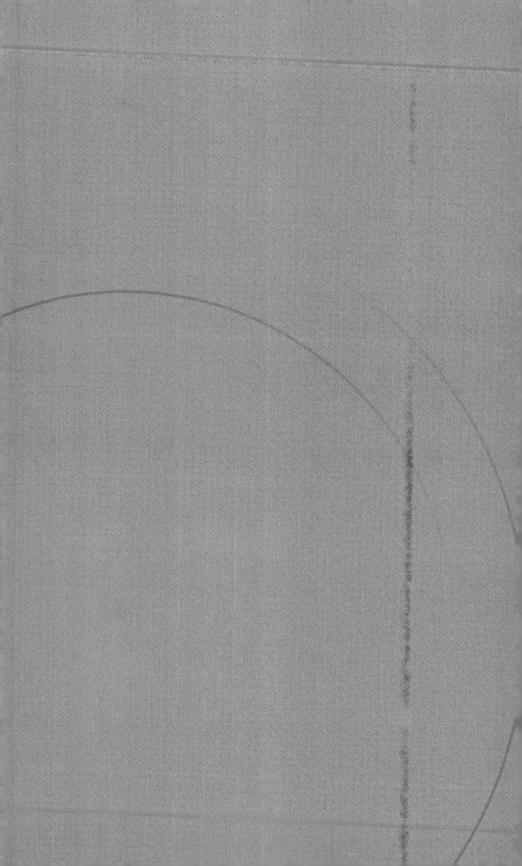

Part 3

The 12 Leadership Derailers

Staller
analysis paralysis

**"You'll never plough a field by
turning it over in your mind."**
Irish proverb.

Over-analysis results in under-delivery. When provided with too many
alternatives, or too much detail, the brain becomes overloaded and can't
move forward. Lifting from the detail releases capacity for decision.

She says

The matter is under review.

She thinks

Consider all information for
the best decision.
Get it right the first time.
You can't rush quality.

He thinks

She needs to make a decision and take action.
She takes too long.
Her team is showing signs of frustration.

Her intention

High quality solid outcome.

360 feedback

- I wish she would just make a decision so I can get on with my work.

- She spends too much time on simple things.

- I feel like her way of working is slowing the rest of us down.

- I am hamstrung. It's frustrating to know that Mary will be involved because I know it will slow things down.

- I think she means well but her need to be 'diligent' is blocking our progress.

DISCOVER – what's the problem?

Chris passed by Mary's office. She was again buried in a pile of paperwork, scowling at the information in front of her. Chris knew Mary had been struggling for some time. She was always behind in her work and seemed to take forever to get anything going. Her in-tray was piled high with small tasks that were just not done. Stuff was getting lost and left behind and things were escalating unnecessarily because Mary was not responding in a timely manner.

Her need to make the right decision meant she was not making any decisions at all. The steering committee is starting to put pressure on Chris to remove Mary from the project. Chris is receiving complaints from other departments who are waiting on outstanding work and can't move forward without Mary's contribution.

DECODE – what's the cause?

MARY

Mary values quality outcomes. She takes pride in her work and likes to take her time to do things right the first time. Mary prefers to gather all the data and thoroughly consider all the options, before taking action or making a decision. She likes to think things through for a while so that she can make the best possible decision.

She's often heard saying that things are "under review".

Mary's intention is to do due diligence to ensure a solid outcome of the highest quality.

The unintended consequences of her preference to take her time to think things through is that she is missing deadlines, her work is piling up, and she is feeling pressured by other people to deliver things before she is ready. She is starting to feel the pressure of letting others down and is worried that she is being overlooked for more important projects as a result.

CHRIS

Mary is spending too much time trying to get things right and not enough time just getting stuff done. Her team is becoming disengaged and frustrated with the speed of her decisions and directions.

Chris suspects it is Mary's reluctance to make decisions that is causing the pile up of her work. Whenever he pushed her for a position or a decision she would request more time. He knew she would then get more research and more information and become more and more stuck in her thinking.

But Chris knew Mary could do the role, she just needed to make quicker decisions to get things back on track. He just hoped she could start building this skill before the committee forced him to remove her from the project.

TEAM

Mary's team is frustrated at her behaviour. They experience her as one big roadblock. Some feel like she can't make decisions and shouldn't be in the role and others see that she is doing her best, has a lot to offer but just suffers from analysis paralysis. Colleagues in other departments know that they will get quality outcomes but will have to wait for them. They balance this up before coming to Mary, and will avoid dealing with her where they can.

SOME POSSIBLE CAUSES

Fear of getting it wrong

Decisions can be risky. To reduce this risk, leaders need to make informed decisions, however information is often unclear, unavailable or insufficient. Without enough information some leaders worry about making bad decisions.

Ironically, this fear of getting it wrong creates a paralysis that almost guarantees a poor result. The longer a leader delays, the more room they make for other issues to take over, including bottlenecks, loss of motivation and increased frustration in others as well as missed opportunities. In the extreme, this behaviour can be perceived by others as perfectionism.

A sea of overwhelm

Decisions need action. A decision is not a decision unless something happens. Up until that time a decision is just a thought. What turns a thought into a decision is the clarity of the next step. Leaders need to know how to break down complex thoughts and analysis and identify the decision required to take the next step.

Leaders who focus on all the information available and get caught up in the complexity of their own thinking, struggle to filter and sort the data in a way that clarifies their next step. This leaves them swirling in a sea of overwhelm, not knowing how to move forward.

Uncomfortable with ambiguity

The decision required is not always clear. Today's business environment is complex, multifaceted and interconnected. This creates a business climate that is always changing and shifting at a rapid pace, requiring a different type of thinking. Decisions in this context are by their very nature ambiguous and uncertain. Leaders who are comfortable with ambiguity are able to make the necessary decisions to operate in this landscape.

Leaders who value certainty or have a preference for black and white thinking struggle to operate comfortably in a world where grey dominates. Never knowing for sure if the decision is right can take an emotional toll on leaders who need a sense of certainty to move forward.

Preference for reflection

Decisions require conviction. At some point the leader needs to be convinced that they have enough data to make a decision, even if it's only for the next step.

Some leaders have a preference for taking their time to become convinced about their decisions. They like to mull over the information before coming to a conclusion. This works well to ensure decisions are robust and not reactive. However, if the leader is unable to adapt their decision-making style to move more quickly when needed, this preference for reflection can grind progress to a halt.

Preference for detail

Decisions need just the right amount of information; no more, no less. The key question is how much is the right amount? Given the answer is as varied as the situations themselves, leaders need to be able to decide when they have enough information to make the best decision possible in the moment. By weighing up the costs of the time taken to improve decisions against the impact of not making the decision quickly enough, the leader can determine how much information is required.

Leaders who have a preference for detail and want to be fully informed before making a decision are at risk of getting this trade-off wrong, potentially causing more issues along the way. Added to that is the risk of more information further confusing the often complex nature of the decision at hand. More information does not always equal more clarity.

Lack of clear objectives

Decisions are made for a reason. Making a decision requires the leader to be clear on the objectives to be achieved. Without knowing the purpose for the decision, leaders can go around in circles trying to make that decision. This can create further confusion for others affected by the decision if the reasoning behind the decision does not fit the objectives.

A lack of clear objectives can also slow down the thinking process, as there are too many open loops to enable an effective decision to be made.

DESIGN – what's the action?

SNAPSHOT OF CURRENT THINKING

Decision-making is recognised as an essential leadership competency for leaders. However, despite an abundance of research on all facets of decision-making, decisions often fail.[38] It is not surprising that leaders often agonise over decision-making. Often over-complicating it or seeking the 'optimal' or 'perfect' solution.

"Decisions are destroyed by over-analysis," says Jeff Stibel, brain scientist and Chairman and CEO of Dun & Bradstreet Credibility Corp. He suggests that "to be frozen by information is perhaps the single biggest risk of knowledge". Leaders who think they need to weigh up every bit of available information against all the potential outcomes take it too far. Stibel states that the leaders who succeed are those who realise that "they'll never have all the answers no matter how much knowledge they gather".[39]

Regular contributor to the *Harvard Business Review*, Ron Ashkenas suggests that consistent with the law of diminishing returns, there is a point where more effort does not produce significant gains. Ashkenas observes that there are two unconscious drivers linked to this behaviour; (1) fear of failure and (2) anxiety about taking action due to avoiding dealing with complex or difficult issues.[40] He concludes that the key to jolting yourself out of analysis paralysis is to view action as a form of research that can inform your future decisions and actions.

The key is to know when you have hit the tipping point of just enough information. But how do we achieve this? Regrettably, researchers have yet to come up with a model that guides us in identifying when we are over-thinking a decision. In her article, *The Paralysis by Analysis*[41], Elizabeth Lovegrove explains how analysis paralysis is a result of the "brain's natural tendency to seize up when confronted with a large number of options that each offer the same cost/reward ratios". The brain has no strategy for resolving the tie breaker, leaving you stuck. She suggests the first and most important step is to "recognise when you are trapped in it" and then, relax, make a plan, narrow down your options, and just do it.

COACHING TIPS TO REDUCE ANALYSIS PARALYSIS

Feel the fear and do it anyway

- Get comfortable with 'near enough is good enough'. Practise this mindset on things that are less important or lower risk to you.

- Act 'as if …' you have the 'right' answer already and you are confident to decide immediately. Act as if you are playing a decision-making game and decide right now.

- Imagine that your quest for quality was creating a reputation for blocking progress. How does this inspire you to move more quickly?

- What are the negative consequences of you continuing to delay making decisions?

- What is the upside of taking a risk?

- Imagine there was no 'wrong'. What would you decide right now?

- Where have you missed an opportunity in the past because you spent too long analysing and failed to make a decision in time? What could you do to avoid that happening again today?

Reduce overwhelm

- When you find yourself overwhelmed with choice and possibility, focus on the first step only and take that action.

- Break the topic down into segments, then decide on the next piece of the smallest segment.
- Step away. Take a walk. Clear your head. Come back later and reconsider.
- Notice how focussing on everything at once causes you to lose sight of the next step. Narrow your focus to a single point only and move forward from there.
- What is the emotional state of 'overwhelm' allowing you to avoid?
- If the statement 'clarity emerges as you engage' were true for you, how could you be a living example of this?
- When analysing the situation, decide what the essential information is and focus on that alone.

Get comfortable with ambiguity

- How can your past experience help you fill in the missing pieces to make a quick decision?
- How does a need for certainty affect your results?
- What is available to you from letting go of the need for certainty?
- What is the downside of certainty?
- Imagine 'black' and 'white' were your enemy, and you loved 'grey'. What would you do next?
- Where in the past did you proceed despite the ambiguity? How could you apply that experience to your current situation?

Increase action

- It's been said that 'no decision' is worse than a 'wrong decision'. How could slow decision-making be impacting your team's productivity and morale?
- When in the past did you take too long to decide and thus missed an opportunity?

- If you could decide based on your first hunch, what would you decide? How can you practise doing more of this?

- What assumptions could you make that would allow you to come to a decision right away?

- What is the difference between reflection and avoidance? What are your triggers for each? Use this to move more quickly.

- What is the minimum amount you need to consider before deciding?

- Decide when you feel half ready – the rest will probably change anyway.

- Action consolidates insights. Take action and the insights will develop progressively.

- If you were to prioritise taking action in a current project, what would you do differently right now?

Reduce detail focus

- List the tasks you do regularly. Rank them in order of the need for high through to low quality/thoroughness. Record the amount of time you typically spend on these tasks. What would have to happen for you to cut these times in half?

- Speak to a colleague or manager who makes decisions without the need for detail. Learn how they do it.

- Assume you have all the detail you need already. What decision would you make?

- If you feel lost in the detail, zoom out and look for the major patterns or principles. Ask yourself what is the purpose of this activity.

- Determine the level of quality required in advance before spending too much time on a task.

- What information do you need in order to really decide?

Ensure clear objectives

- What is this decision really about?
- What are the three key objectives that need to be satisfied in making this decision?
- What is the purpose of making this decision?
- Why does this decision matter? Keep this top of mind as you analyse and decide.
- What else do you need to know about the objectives in order to have a clear framework for decision-making?

SUMMARY

- Work grinds to a halt.
- The prevailing perception is information over action.
- The direct report's driving intention is quality outcomes.
- Possible drivers? They may fear getting it wrong, be overwhelmed by too much information, stumble with grey. They like thinking a decision through fully. They want and need more detail and they lack clear objectives for decision-making.

Controller
command and control

"The greatest form of power is the power to control one's self not the power to control others."
Unknown

Directing may secure compliance, but not ownership and commitment. Command and control does not translate across all leadership scenarios and may disengage team members. A coaching approach will enlist others in their own outcomes, inspire discretionary effort, and build team capacity

She says

Do it <u>this</u> way.

She thinks

I need to keep a tight rein on this.
If I don't tell them they won't know.
There is no time to watch and learn.
My job is to provide clear instruction.

He thinks

There's no consultation.
Her team is becoming demotivated.
I'm concerned by the number of bullying complaints.
Mary is stressed and not handling the workload.

Her intention

Control a quality outcome.

360 feedback

- She's a big bully.

- Mary won't listen to any of our ideas. I just shut up now and do what I am told – little care and no responsibility.

- She doesn't trust me to do my work well.

- Because of her I am trying to get out. I would have left already but I can't afford to.

- She is a bottleneck – we have to wait for her for decisions, even on stuff we know well, maybe better than her.

- Loves the sound of her own voice. She is always telling me stuff I already know.

- As innovative as a block of concrete.

- Mary would do well in the military where she could happily direct people all day.

- Mary? A constant barrage of criticism!

DISCOVER – what's the problem?

Mary's strength of character appealed to Chris immediately when they met for her first interview. She was articulate, clear on what was required and highly committed to getting a good outcome. She started strongly, quickly bringing a sense of order to a team that had been neglected and descended into chaos before her arrival.

Now nine months later, the chaos had been transformed into order and yet this was accompanied by a loss of innovation and a team culture oscillating between fear and resentment. Mary's staff engagement scores were the lowest of the whole corporate centre.

The Occupational Health and Safety Manager had just advised Chris there had been a second complaint of bullying against Mary and 'strongly advised' Chris to get involved and sort it out.

DECODE – what's the cause?

MARY

Mary values clarity and order. She believes that staff will be motivated if they know exactly what needs to be done. She sees her role as providing that clarity through clear and specific instruction, and then ensuring that the standard has been maintained.

Mary has observed other colleagues on the leadership team using a coaching style, which she judges as being risky – even weak. Mary enjoys the power of her leadership position and is comfortable exercising that power. She believes that ensuring a consistent quality requires her to be very explicit in her instructions and vigilant in their implementation.

She's often heard saying, "Just do it this way". "If I don't tell them they won't know," is a regular response to Chris.

Mary's intention is to ensure a quality outcome.

The unintended consequences of her preference to maintain close control is that she is beginning to feel out of control personally with the amount she has to do. She feels that if she could just get on top of the workload, things would be okay.

Mary knows that her team believes she isn't consulting them sufficiently. Consultation takes time, and there's so much to be done already. The responsibility of being delegated the authority to lead the team rests heavily on her shoulders.

CHRIS

Chris values Mary's strength and work ethic. He used to value what he saw as her strong leadership, and now he is beginning to question if it really is leadership. It was clear that Mary had no flexibility in her style – command and control or nothing. Chris had often heard the phrase 'my way or the high way', but until Mary he had never really understood what that meant!

Until recently Mary seemed very happy, and now she was looking stressed and tired. Mary's need to direct everything had created bottlenecks that were slowing everything down. Chris had overheard conversations between Mary and various members of her team. Mary was so intense, spoke clearly and sharply, and there was little evidence of warmth or willingness to enter discussion. When added to the power differential caused by her title, unfortunately the claims of bullying did not surprise him.

TEAM

Mary's team is ready to mutiny. When she first arrived they liked that she seemed to know what needed to happen and was happy to step up and take control. Now they realise she only has one strategy – command and control. A few are looking for new roles both within and outside the company but the job market is tight. Others are simply bored. There is general consensus in the team that she doesn't trust anyone except herself, and has no tolerance for even the slightest variation from her plan.

Many think Mary is a bully and a couple have lodged formal complaints. Two of the more generous team members think she may be afraid of losing control.

SOME POSSIBLE CAUSES

Strong need to check everything

Checking up on delegated work is a valuable leadership behaviour. Trusting your team to get the work done creates the conditions for team members to make autonomous contributions. A leader who does not trust the team, and who needs to check everything, will stifle creativity and engagement within their team. This will often create bottlenecks, high workloads and a struggle to achieve work-life balance for the leader.

High detail focus

Detail is important. The right level of detail is even more important. As a leader progresses up the corporate ladder, less detail and more 'big picture' thinking is required. A leader who is motivated to work sequentially through tasks and/or take a detailed approach can find it challenging to empower others as they may feel uncomfortable without detailed knowledge of the task.

Desire for sole responsibility

Accountability is at the heart of leadership. Balancing being in control and having full responsibility with releasing control is a paradox of leadership. A leader who wants sole responsibility for the work may hold tightly onto control, increasing their own anxiety while disempowering their people. This behaviour could be viewed by others as demanding, dominating and/or directive.

Critical of colleagues who they regard as not taking responsibility for their section of the work, they may be seen as self-focused, controlling or not motivated to delegate or collaborate.

High need for personal achievement

Performance is important. As a leader, the performance of the team matters more than your individual performance. A leader who is overly focused on their own achievement may take over the work of others to ensure that their high standards are maintained, resulting in disempowerment and/or disengagement.

The desire for recognition of the results they have achieved may also limit this leader's ability to share the workload and the recognition. Their high standards for themselves and others may result in them driving themselves too hard and being reluctant to delegate.

High need for power

Power is central to leadership. Being comfortable with your own authority as a leader is crucial for ensuring people follow you. An overly high need to have or display power can damage relationships and reduce team productivity. Leaders who constantly exert their power over others stifle creativity and limit responsibility in their people, resulting in disengagement.

DESIGN – what's the action?

SNAPSHOT OF CURRENT THINKING

Insights gained from the field of psychology have revealed that while we notice many traits in other people, the traits of warmth and strength are the most influential. These two traits "account for more than 90% of the variance in our positive or negative impressions"[42] of the people around us.

In their *Harvard Business Review* article entitled, 'Connect, Then Lead', Amy Cuddy, Matthew Kohut and John Neffinger pose the question of whether it is better for leaders to be warm or strong. They comment that most leaders will try to highlight their strength, competence and credentials. This can lead to "a host of unresourceful behaviours" and inhibit cognitive functioning of employees, causing them to disengage. Drawing upon an extensive body of research, they conclude that leaders must start with warmth, as this is the most effective approach. It is the "conduit of influence"[43] as it generates trust, open communication and creative thinking. Added to this is the fact that people consistently pick up warmth faster than competence as found by Princeton social psychologist Alex Todorov.[44] This means that it is important for leaders to earn the right to command by first connecting with their employees. Strength and capability alone do not guarantee engagement.

Uncertainty is a common experience in our 21st century workforces. Cuddy, Kohut and Neffinger state that people will be more tolerant of uncertainty when they feel they have a leader who "has their back, and is calm, clearheaded and courageous".[45] Therefore, a leadership style of constant command and control, while initially providing an antidote to the environmental uncertainty, over time will likely serve to undermine the value of this certainty.

An overly directive leadership style can cause others to distance themselves and disconnect from the leader. Research from Naomi Eisenberger and Matthew Liberman from UCLA suggests that a lack of feeling connected to others causes what we call social pain.[46] Social pain can produce symptoms that are similar to physical pain. This was reflected through their studies of the brain showing that "some of the same brain regions that respond to physical pain also respond to social pain".[47] The researchers also found that taking the pain-killer Tylenol reduced the feelings of social hurt.[48] Social pain is as real as physical pain and can be experienced at the extreme end of command and control leadership.

COACHING TIPS TO REDUCE YOUR RELIANCE ON COMMAND AND CONTROL LEADERSHIP

Know what needs checking and let the rest go

- What message are you sending your team by your need to check everything and remain in control?

- What do you appreciate about being trusted with a new activity/ project that challenges you and develops your skills? How does your team experience your trust?

- What steps can you take to incrementally build your trust in your team and reduce the need to check everything?

- Who else could do this? How could it support them to grow? How would getting others more involved and giving them responsibility free you up to provide team leadership rather than task leadership?

- Is holding onto all the work actually improving the quality of your outcomes as intended? What is the unintended consequence of this?

- Wherever possible, if a team member feels uncomfortable with the task, take the time to support them and help them learn rather than take back the task.

Reduce detail focus

- What are the essential concepts you need to focus on, that can then allow you to delegate the activity and allow others to complete the work their way?

- How can you trust you have all the detail you need already, to zoom out of the detail more often, so you can delegate confidently and then let go?

- Understand that you can present the overview, knowing you don't need to be in control of everything. Your team can provide detailed knowledge when needed.

- Consider a leader in your organisation who is well respected and yet not always across the detail. What can you learn from them?

Allow others to take responsibility

- A command and control approach is absolutely appropriate in some settings – for example in an emergency. A Fire Brigade Incident Controller would appropriately use this style on a fire ground. He would not use this style effectively in the team debrief after the emergency has been resolved. Where might you be inappropriately sticking to a command and control style when a more collaborative approach may generate better results?

- What is the personal cost to you for holding on to so much work? What is the professional cost to your reputation as someone who leads in a command and control style?

- What else could you achieve if you cut your workload by 30 per cent due to delegating more and letting others take responsibility? What does your company expect you to be achieving?

- What outcome do you need? What is the minimum amount of responsibility you need to take so you can delegate this task?

- Delegate responsibility and authority, not just the task.

- Who else needs to learn this? What's the benefit to them if they do it from now on? What's the benefit to you in the long run?

- Set a definite task completion date and a follow-up system. Set a deadline and check in points along the way to make sure everything is on track. Offer your assistance if it's needed and then step back.

Reduce need for personal achievement and focus on team achievement

- Know that in a leadership role, you are judged by how well you develop your team—the collective performance—and less on your personal performance. How will that knowledge influence how you empower your team?

- Do three things every day this week to show warmth and appreciation to your peers for their achievements. Review your outcomes at the end of the week to determine which you will continue next week.

- Imagine a spoilt child wanting to be the centre of attention at a birthday party. Imagine it's possible that you are displaying that type of behaviour in the adult form. How can increasing delegation shift that perception?

- Give public and written credit when work is delegated and done well. Notice the impact this has on team morale, as well as motivation and job satisfaction on an individual basis.

- Any time you feel proud of yourself for a job well done, congratulate someone else and monitor the impact on their engagement.

Reduce your need for power

- Imagine for a moment that warmth is much more important than competence to lead and influence others. What would you do differently?

- Before you assert an opinion or a command, ask a question. Do this consistently for a week and notice what changes.

- Practice a ratio of three questions for every instruction you give. Always include one question about the other person's perspective or opinion.

- Recognise that the leadership role you have carries an inherent power that others acknowledge. How can you let that power speak for itself?

- Ghandi is now acknowledged as one of history's most powerful leaders, and yet in watching him you would not have seen any overt exercise of power. What could you learn from Ghandi and apply today?

- People like don't to be told. Try asking instead of telling to build greater engagement and a sense of connection.

SUMMARY

- Staff feels bullied.
- The prevailing perception is 'their way or the highway'.
- The direct report's driving intention is clarity and order.
- Possible drivers? They have a strong need to check everything; a desire for the detail; are motivated by accountability and a need for personal performance or power.

Cyclone
bull at a gate

"Take time for all things:
great haste makes great waste."
Benjamin Franklin

Go slow to go fast. Acting without consideration can leave collateral damage. The leader who acts boldly with caution brings followers along the journey.

She says

Let's make this happen.

She thinks

Seize the opportunity.
Action precedes clarity.
I don't want to miss out.
I want to get the result now.
I learn best on the go.

He thinks

Where's her due diligence?
She leaves people behind.
There's a disconnect between Mary and her team.
She often creates rework.

Her intention

Get results.

360 feedback

- She rushes into things without seeking input and wonders why we don't support the plan!

- We all have to go into repair mode afterwards because she didn't plan for what could go wrong!

- It is exhausting working in this team – she changes her mind so fast and we are expected to make it happen.

- So much wasted effort!

- Love her energy but wish she had a volume control.

- Not sure who will burn out first – her or us!

DISCOVER – what's the problem?

If this wasn't his leadership team, Chris would have found the situation amusing! Mary had raced off ahead again – in her mind the goal was clear, decisions were made, and she was ready to take action. She seemed oblivious to the fact that the rest of the team still needed to debate the key issues and were not ready to make a decision. Mary was keen to implement and the rest of the group were still scoping the issue.

Chris suspected this was what was happening in Mary's team too. He was noticing signs that members of her team were disengaged. Last week one of Mary's key people expressed that he didn't know why they were doing what they were doing – Mary just expected them to take action. There is also concern that Mary lacks a clear vision and does not think through the key issues before commencing. The team seems to be fatigued by Mary's frequent change in direction as they adjust to her latest thinking.

DECODE – what's the cause?

MARY

Mary values action, and takes pride in her ability to think on her feet. She focuses on getting things done and is always keen to seize an opportunity there and then. She knows that sometimes other people find her constant action tiring. On the flip side she is frustrated by their need to talk things through for so long, and the delay this introduces to projects.

"Let's make this happen" is one of her favourite sayings! Preferring to learn on the job, Mary can often be heard saying, "Action precedes clarity" when others are not sure what action to take.

Mary's intention is to get results. She knows if she takes action quickly she can usually avoid feeling overwhelmed and work things out as she goes.

Mary does have a secret fear of not wanting to miss out. She also wonders if she might be at risk of burnout, but she loves the adrenalin hit and wouldn't have it any other way. The unintended consequences of her approach include risking leaving her team behind when she doesn't take the time to explain her vision and why she is proposing a particular course of action. Others can judge her willingness to change position midstream as a lack of responsibly and forethought, creating concern about Mary's unwillingness to consider risks before taking action.

CHRIS

Chris values Mary's high initiative approach, and appreciates her energy and the can-do attitude she brings to the team. At her best she is the spark the rest of the team needs, yet at her worst she is like a bull at a gate, rushing into things before thinking them through.

Chris's major concern is Mary's lack of due diligence and her apparent unwillingness to take the time to develop and communicate a conceptual vision before commencing action. This often results in a disconnect between Mary and her team, or Mary and the rest of the leadership team.

Chris had an opportunity to take Mary to a board meeting recently, but decided he couldn't risk her committing to action without thought. Her tendencies are beginning to have a detrimental impact on her career possibilities.

TEAM

Mary's team admire her constant energy, and yet most of them can't keep up with her and don't want to. Time is wasted within the team trying to decipher the strategy from Mary's instructions, as it's very rare that she provides a contextual backdrop for projects.

A couple of more risk averse members of Mary's team experience her as irresponsible as she seems to refuse to think things through before taking action. The constant change of direction is exhausting – Mary is happy to think while taking action and her lack of communication about changes and adjustments along the way results in rework and waste in the team.

SOME POSSIBLE CAUSES

Overly strong goal focus

Focusing on goals at the expense of risk can be dangerous. A strong goal focus, balanced with the ability to anticipate and mitigate risk, is necessary for success and moderates immediate and ill-considered action.

A leader who is so energised by focusing on goals, may overlook the potential risks or problems that may be encountered on the pathway to achieving the goal. They may feel frustrated or annoyed by people who direct their attention to potential obstacles, leading to disconnection within their team. Their strong goal focus may also cause them to be surprised by problems that arise, even though these problems were obvious to others, and possibly even communicated to them in advance.

Taking action too quickly

Making wise decisions is a key role of leadership. Outside an emergency, acting first and thinking later risks leaving your followers behind.

A leader who is energised by taking immediate action without pause for reflection could appear to others as someone who wants to move forward too quickly with a tendency to 'act first and think later'. Others may judge them as impatient to commence activity, prone to disorganisation, or lacking in vision.

'Just do it' summarises their approach to new projects or tasks as they believe they can work things out as they go along. They may waste energy by not properly understanding, planning or communicating their strategy or plan before making a start. It may be hard for this leader to agree when others ask for more time to think things through.

Team members are likely to feel left behind, or lacking a conceptual framework for activity.

They may generate a lot of activity which is only associated with getting started on new projects, rather than following things through to completion, leaving a trail of unfinished activity.

Deciding quickly

Leaders need to strike a balance between speed and accuracy. Decisions made too quickly without appropriate considerations may not accommodate management of risk.

A leader who makes rapid decisions may appear to others as someone who is rash, hasty and ill considered. They may later look back on a decision and regret it, wondering how they came to that decision. This could lead them to re-deciding on another pathway. This making and remaking of decisions can be confusing and exhausting for team members and stakeholders.

Due to their ability to make quick decisions, this leader may fail to validate the work involved from others in developing and presenting concepts for decision, and can leave others feeling unappreciated.

DESIGN – what's the action?

SNAPSHOT OF CURRENT THINKING

The *Oxford Dictionary* defines the phrase 'bull at a gate' as, "taking action hastily and without thought."

Leaders are expected to be agile in their decision-making but also need to strike a balance between speed and accuracy to make decisions that accommodate management of risk. Research conducted at Vanderbilt University suggests that the brain switches into a different mode when it is forced to act quickly, essentially trading off accuracy for speed.[49] "So, even though the brain might be presented with the exact same information, if the decision is made under speed stress, the problem will be analysed differently than it would be under accuracy stress." Therefore, the opportunity for error is higher.

Decision-making is already challenging, not only because of complex working environments but also because of the complexity of our brain's functioning. Leaders like to think they are rational in their decision-making. However we are all prone to hundreds of proven cognitive biases that cause us to think and act irrationally while believing we are being rational. Daniel Kahneman won the Nobel Prize in Economics arising from his study on how often we do irrational things.[50] For example, we tend to listen only to the information that confirms our preconceptions. Known as confirmation bias, it also has a close cousin known as the observer-expectancy effect, where our expectations unconsciously influence our perception of an outcome. With an explanation of just these two biases, it is easy to see how our version of reality may become skewed in relation to others' perceptions.

Bull-at-a-gate behaviour provides an open playing field for these cognitive influences to have free rein. When deciding quickly, they don't take enough time to gather information and explore options. Consequently, leaders can create chaos for their team members when they head in one direction, and then shortly after switch to another or better idea (and it is likely to occur more than just once). There is waste involved in this approach.

There is also a detrimental impact for the leader, who can lose credibility and the engagement of their team members, who can suffer burnout from the 'start, stop, change' approach.

Leadership and management expert, Dan Rockwell[51], recommends the following six steps to minimise flip-flop decision-making caused by haste:

- Listen and ask questions. John Wooden (American basketball player and coach) said, "Go slow to go fast".

- Consider the impact of your decision on all parties.

- Talk through your decisions privately before going public.

- Stay the course unless important factors change.

- Focus more on targets and less on methods.

- Make minor course corrections that keep you on target.

COACHING TIPS TO REDUCE BULL-AT-A-GATE BEHAVIOUR

Reduce an overly strong goal focus

- Exercise more caution and consider the worst case scenario and then use this to inform your action.

- What are the risks associated with this endeavour? Who could you involve in determining the next steps to ensure these risks are managed?

- If you were to overlook the risks, what is the likely outcome? Why is it important to address and minimise these risks?

- What contingency plans can you put in place to mitigate your highest identified risk in this project/task?

- Get your team together and brainstorm everything that could go wrong with this activity.

- Imagine your success depended on you working with your team to find five potential problems with this plan. Do that now.

Pause before taking action

- If you were to prioritise developing and communicating a conceptual understanding of your current project before taking action, what would you do differently right now?

- Why is it important that this task is completed? How does it contribute to your organisation's objectives?

- Metaphors are one type of conceptual thinking that can engage a team. If you were to describe your activities in a metaphor, what would that metaphor be?

- Imagine you are a newspaper sub-editor. Write a one-sentence conceptual headline about why you are completing each project you are involved in. How would knowing this help your team connect to the purpose of the activity?

- Before starting any task, get clear on the purpose. Write yourself a statement about why you are doing it. Try out sharing this statement on your team.

- When you are preparing for a meeting with someone, get clear on the three key points you want to make and why they are important.

- Imagine that creating action would set off a serious allergy. What would you do instead?

- When you think you've got enough information to get started, pause and find out more.

- Have a colleague peer review your intended course of action and share their reflections before you take action.

- To prevent wasting time on the wrong activity, outline how you will plan and prioritise your actions, and then structure and organise your resources and time before taking action.

- Make minor course corrections that keep you on target, and communicate these to your team and/or key stakeholders.

Deciding rigorously

- When making this decision, what new and valuable insights will be available to you, if you allow an additional period of time before deciding?

- When in the past have you allowed a period of time to pass before making a decision, and it improved the outcome?

- What question can you ask yourself to prevent an immediate decision, give you reflection time and sure up the proof before deciding?

- Think of a time in the past when you made an immediate decision and later regretted it. What was the insight you gained from the passage of time?

- From experience, how much time do you need to make this decision, in order to get the best outcome? For the next three weeks, double the period of time you take and notice the resulting quality of your decision-making.

- Canvas the opinions of others and consider the new perspectives before finalising your decision.

- When you have received the necessary information, test the veracity of the facts and information against a number of different sources before making a decision.

SUMMARY

- Staff feel puzzled and left behind.
- The prevailing perception is action without consideration.
- The direct report's driving intention is to think while taking action.
- Possible drivers? They may have a strong goal focus; they take action too quickly; they prioritise speed over accuracy.

Doer
can't delegate

"No man will make a great leader who wants to do
it all himself, or to get all the credit for doing it."
Andrew Carnegie

Delegation is a productivity multiplier. We are seduced into thinking that
by doing things ourselves we are saving time and improving quality. The
more we can let go of the work we do and empower others to do it, the
more we collectively get done.

She says

I'll just do it myself.

She thinks
My team is too swamped already.
No one can do this as well as I can.
I don't want to get it wrong.
It's quicker to do it myself.
There's no one else to do it.

He thinks

She can't cope.
She's not cut out for the job.
She's not a good role model for her team.
She's a bottleneck.
She impacts work quality and deadlines.

Her intention
Quality outcome.

360 feedback

- Mary doesn't trust me. Actually, I don't think she trusts any of us.

- I'm bored and I am not developing any new skills.

- She's difficult to approach because she's too busy.

- She gets overwhelmed with stuff that doesn't matter.

- Mary doesn't know the difference between being a leader and an analyst.

- She withholds all the good work for herself.

- She's creating a bottleneck that we can't fix.

DISCOVER – what's the problem?

It's Monday morning and Chris scans his inbox: another 20 emails from Mary over the weekend. The top email is about the EastBourne Project. Chris suggested to Mary, "Why not get Loretta to lead this one? She's got the expertise." Chris could have predicted what came next: "Loretta has a huge workload right now. I will take care of it." He looks across the office and sees Mary's team; probably all working on menial tasks.

This has to stop. Mary's inability to delegate is stifling the development of the team and affecting her productivity. Even with all the extra hours she's putting in to keep on top of things, the quality of her work is slipping and she is often stressed and short-tempered.

Chris knows the organisation can't afford to lose more people. He is worried that Mary is not developing her team and therefore in danger of not only losing them, but not developing the leadership bench strength to take the company forward.

DECODE – what's the cause?

MARY

Mary is swamped with work. She likes the idea of delegating more work to her team but finds the reality challenging. It's much quicker to just do the work herself, and there's also the added bonus of ensuring the quality is up to scratch if she does it herself. It takes a long time to show someone what she wants and by the time she's done she could have completed the task herself anyway.

She knows too, that even if she were to delegate more, she could be causing undue stress to her team members as they are also under the pump and she feels guilty piling up more work on them. And anyway, she's tried delegating before but that created a disaster, which took her twice as long to fix up afterwards.

She's often heard describing a task and then finishing off with, "Actually don't worry about it, it'll be easier if I just do it myself." In her most honest moments, Mary admits to herself that she is a little anxious about being upstaged by some of her team members.

Mary's intention is to ensure a quality outcome.

The unintended consequences of her preference to do things herself rather than delegate them is that she is in overwhelm. She has too much to do and not enough time to get it done. This is affecting the quality of her work and she is missing deadlines. Not only has her productivity suffered but she is also noticing some changes within her team. People seem to be lacking motivation and are not stepping up. She has also noticed a reluctance among her peers on the leadership team to include her in strategic conversations.

Mary begins to feel downright miserable when she thinks about her home life. Her husband has been making unhelpful comments about her need to introduce herself to her teenage sons, and her mother is complaining that Mary never comes to visit.

CHRIS

Chris values Mary's dedication and commitment. He is also concerned that she is not coping. She appears to be struggling to handle the workload and things are being missed, and yet she is not delegating to her team. Mary also appears unaware of how her lack of delegation is actually impacting team morale. Some members of her team are talking to other managers about working for them as they are not being developed in their current roles.

Bottom line is that Mary and her team are not as productive as they should be, and perhaps this results from Mary still seeing herself as a 'doer' rather than a leader?

Chris also wonders if Mary would feel irrelevant/replaceable if others could do her job as well as she can. As it stands Chris is reluctant to give Mary any stretch goals as he's not convinced that Mary is even suitable for the role she is in right now.

TEAM

Mary's team are demoralised. They are languishing in their roles without sufficient challenge to keep them engaged and stretched. Some are frustrated and feel resentful that Mary is holding onto all the interesting work and only letting them do the simple tasks. Others are simply bored. There is general consensus in the team that she doesn't trust any of them. Most find it hard to approach Mary about the situation because she seems overwhelmed and too busy to spend time with them.

Those most passionate about the success of the organisation find Mary's approach hardest to bear – they believe her management style will soon impact on the organisational brand.

SOME POSSIBLE CAUSES

Unwilling to invest in delegation

Dedicating the time needed to define the activity and develop others is crucial to delegation. A leader who does not invest in developing their team will always struggle to delegate and will wear the consequences of workload.

This trait can appear to others as lacking in trust or being unwilling to develop the team.

Low trust in the team to deliver a quality output

Trust in the capability of the people you work with enables delegation. A leader who does not trust the team is likely to struggle to delegate when driven by the need to guarantee consistent and quality results and a belief that no one can do the job as well as they do. This will often translate into high workloads and a struggle to achieve work-life balance.

High detail focus

As a leader progresses up the corporate ladder, less detail and more big-picture thinking is required. A leader who is motivated to work sequentially through tasks and/or take a detailed approach can appear to be micromanaging. This leader may prefer to work from the bottom up and focus on the individual details that make up the whole.

This leader could appear to be focusing energy on things that are not strategically important, or seeking involvement in everything so they feel across the topic. This leader may also find delegation challenging, as they may feel uncomfortable letting go of the detailed knowledge.

High need for personal achievement and/or recognition

As a participant, your own performance is important. As a leader, the performance of the team matters more. A leader who is overly focused on their own achievement may take over the work of others to ensure that their high standards are maintained. The desire for recognition of the results they have achieved may also limit the ability to share the workload.

Need for control

Balancing being in control with releasing control is a paradox of leadership. A leader who holds tightly onto control risks increasing their own anxiety while disempowering their people. A leader with an excessive need to be in charge could be viewed by others as demanding, dominating and/or directive.

A high need for control will foster micromanagement and thwart the ability to delegate due to the belief that no one can do the job as well as they do. This will often translate into high workloads and a struggle to achieve work-life balance. Critical of colleagues who they regard as not taking sufficient responsibility for the quality/timeliness of the work, they may be seen as self-focused or controlling or not motivated to collaborate.

Redefining identity from technician to leader

Moving into a leadership role requires a shift in identity, typically from 'technician' (or 'doer') to leader. A leader who does not make this transition may end up with an inner conflict over the definition of their role, how to carry it out and what constitutes success.

Their desire to be seen as 'part of the team', rather than a 'management overhead', may create reluctance to delegate. They may be so used to 'doing' that 'thinking', 'strategising' or 'planning' doesn't seem to be a valid use of their time. They may not yet feel they have the authority to hand out work. They may also fear that if the team knows how to do things, they themselves could become redundant. All these beliefs can limit the ability to distribute work.

DESIGN – what's the action?

SNAPSHOT OF CURRENT THINKING

"The surest way for an executive to kill himself is to refuse to learn how, and when, and to whom to delegate work," said James Cash Penney[52], founder of the J.C. Penney retail chain. A 2007 study on time management conducted by the Institute for Corporate Productivity (i4cp) found that 46 per cent of the 332 companies surveyed were concerned about their employees' delegation skills.[53] Delegation is a fundamental activity to keep the right level of work at the right level of the organisation. Employees need to be working on things that stretch and develop them and pave the way for career development. Delegation therefore is not just a tool for growth, but a strategy for retention and engagement for both the leader and the person they are leading.

London Business School Professor Julian Birkinshaw and productivity expert Jordan Cohen spent three years studying how knowledge workers could become more productive. They found the simple answer was to: "Eliminate or delegate unimportant tasks and replace them with value-added ones". Their research indicates "that knowledge workers spend a great deal of their time, an average of 41%, on discretionary activities that offer little personal satisfaction and could be handled competently by others.[54] Birkinshaw and Cohen found that their study participants delegated from 2 to 20 per cent of their work with no decline in team productivity.

Jan Yager, in her book *Work Less, Do More*, outlines several key steps for effective delegation:

- **Choose what tasks you are willing to delegate.** You should be doing the most critical business tasks and those that only you can do. Delegate what you can't do, and what doesn't interest you.

- **Pick the best person to delegate to.** Best means the person who is most likely to deliver, with the right skill level.

- **Trust those to whom you delegate.** It always starts with trust and provides the team member an opportunity to do the task their own way unless absolutely necessary.

- **Give clear assignments and instructions.** The key is striking the right balance between too much detail and not enough.

- **Set a definite task completion date and a follow-up system.** Set a deadline and check-in points along the way to make sure everything is on track.

- **Give public and written credit.** Often overlooked or forgotten, this action will increase employee motivation and job satisfaction.

- **Delegate responsibility and authority, not just the task.**

- **Avoid reverse delegation, provide guidance and feedback when needed.** Wherever possible, if a team member feels uncomfortable with the task, take the time to support them and help them learn rather than take back the task.

Birkinshaw and Cohen's study would add that 'timing matters'. In the words of one participant, "I learned about the importance of timing in delegating something – it is possible to delegate too early".

COACHING TIPS TO INCREASE THE ABILITY TO DELEGATE

Create time by delegating

- What if 'taking time' was actually 'buying time'? What could you spend the extra time on in the long run?

- If you considered the time you need to delegate as an 'investment' and not a 'cost', what could shift for you?

- If your status quo on delegation is maintained, what are the implications for your career development and that of your team members?

- Pick the best person to delegate to. Best means the person who is most likely to deliver, with the right skill level. Delegate and agree on the next check-in point.

- Imagine that delegation could give you a gift of an extra half a day a week. What are you willing to shift to secure that gift?

Trust the team can deliver a quality output

- What kind of leader do you imagine yourself to be? Or strive to be? How do they develop their people? What do they delegate through trust?

- Who else needs to learn what you know? What's the immediate benefit to them and to you if they have that knowledge from now on? What are the long-term benefits?

- What message are you sending your team by doing the majority of the work?

- How could your team members perceive this act, even if it's not your intention?

- What do you appreciate about being trusted with a new activity/ project that challenges you and develops your skills? How is your team experiencing your trust?

- What steps can you take to incrementally build your trust in your team?

- Who else could do this task you are about to do now? How could it support them to grow?

- Make a decision to trust those to whom you delegate, and then provide an opportunity for them to do the task.

- Is holding on to all the work actually improving the quality of your outcomes as you're intending? How can you be sure? What would your line manager say?

- Wherever possible, if a team member feels uncomfortable with the task, take the time to support them and help them learn rather than take back the task.

Reduce detail focus

- What are the essential concepts you need to focus on, that can then allow you to delegate the activity?

- Free yourself to embrace a broader perspective by surrounding yourself with people who can competently manage the detail and deliver on activity.

- What are the essential concepts you need to retain focus on? Allow yourself to delegate the rest.

- How can you trust you have all the detail you need already so that you can step back and loosen the reins, and allow the person to get on with the task?

- The Pareto principle states that 80 per cent of the effects come from 20 per cent of the causes. The detail of 80 per cent of your work won't matter. What's the 20 per cent you need to focus on? What can you delegate to your team?

- What is the current cost to you of working continually with this level of detail? Consider the cost personally, for your team and for the organisation.

- Act 'as if …' you didn't need any of the detail, and allow your team members to know it and take ownership of the activity. You know where to find them if you need them.

- List the tasks you do regularly. Rank them in order of the need for high through to low quality/thoroughness. Assume you need to delegate half this activity to your people. Which half will it be?

- Speak to a colleague or manager who successfully delegates. Learn how they let go of the detail.

Reduce need for personal achievement

- Imagine a spoilt child wanting to be the centre of attention at a birthday party. Is it possible that you are displaying that type of behaviour in the adult form? How can increasing delegation shift that perception?

- Set a definite task completion date and a follow-up system. Set a deadline and check-in points along the way to make sure everything is on track. Offer your assistance if it's needed and then step back.

- Give public and written credit when work is delegated and done well. Notice the impact this has on team morale, as well as motivation and job satisfaction on an individual basis.

- What else could you achieve if you cut your workload by 30 per cent due to delegating more? What does your company expect you to be achieving?

- If you were to increase the overall productivity of your team through successful delegation, what would be the impact on your personal reputation?

Allow others control

- What is the personal cost to you for holding on to so much work? What is the professional cost to your reputation as someone who holds on to work?

- Ask yourself "Who is ready to be developed into my role? How am I supporting this growth?" Use your responses to guide your delegation.

- What outcome do you need? What is the minimum amount of involvement you need to delegate this task?

- Delegate responsibility and authority – not just the task.

Redefine identity from technician to leader

- As a person becomes more senior in an organisation, with broader responsibilities and competing demands on their time, they typically become less detailed and more 'big picture'. What detail do you need to let go of to move from being a technician to a leader?

- What is the employment cost per hour to do your role? Should the company be spending $xx p/h on the tasks you are not delegating to others?

- What's the lowest level of the organisation that your tasks need to sit at?

- Keep a log of the tasks you do each day. At the end of the week, review the list for the tasks that come up often and can be delegated. List the people who need to be able to do those tasks. Make a commitment to delegate those tasks from now on to everyone on that list. Repeat this process until you are only doing tasks appropriate for your role.

- Compare your job description now with the job description you had in a sub-leadership role. What new competencies are required? How might your reluctance to delegate be getting in the way of your developing these new competencies?

- Choose what tasks you are willing to delegate. You should be doing the most critical business tasks and those that only you can do. Delegate what you can't do, and what doesn't interest you.

SUMMARY

- Workflow is bottlenecked.

- The prevailing perception is that staff are underdeveloped and untrusted.

- The direct report's driving intention is quality outcomes.

- Possible drivers? They may be unwilling to invest in delegation; have low trust in the team; have a high focus on the detail; a need for personal achievement; a need for control; they still see themselves as a technician not a leader.

Avoider
conflict averse

**"Honest disagreement is often
a good sign of progress."**
Mahatma Gandhi

Burying your head in the sand does not make the problem go away.
Avoiding a difficult conversation pushes problems underground.
Creative conflict is the catalyst for building stronger relationships and
harnessing different perspectives to generate well-rounded solutions.

She says

That's ok.
Let's just see how it goes.

She thinks

I don't like conflict.
I don't want to rock the boat.
A happy team is a productive team.
Conflict is bad.

He thinks

She's tolerating poor behaviour.
She's not having tough conversations.
She appears as a weak leader.
Others are taking advantage because
they know there is no recourse.

Her intention

Keep the peace and protect relationships.

360 feedback

- Mary is such a gentle person. She wouldn't hurt a fly. I just wish she would hold some of our team members to account more.

- Mary is great to work for. She basically gives you free rein to do whatever you like! It's very relaxed. She's always cool if you don't get stuff done. It makes for a very cruisy job.

- Mary is very nice but I'm starting to get really annoyed that I seem to be the only one who does any real work around here. Why doesn't she tell people off when they are out of line? It's driving me crazy.

- The other day we received an email from HR about not wearing open-toed shoes to client meetings, yet the next week there were three women who were wearing sandals! What's the point of policies if they are never reinforced?? Sandals are unprofessional.

- I never know if I've really done a good job because Mary finds something good in everyone's work.

- I don't feel like I'm getting enough critical feedback to develop key skills. I want someone to just give it to me straight!

DISCOVER – what's the problem?

Mary had asked Chris to support her in having the tough conversation with Frank, one of her team members who was having issues with colleagues. She had avoided addressing this situation for a few months now but was unable to avoid it any longer. Chris had confronted her with the situation and asked what she was going to do about it. She had reluctantly said she would speak to Frank about it, but never did. And now it had come to this.

There had been two complaints lodged about Frank's behaviour in the last week and now they were having the 'formal' discussion. Mary was very uncomfortable and was skirting around the edges of the topic, trying to keep it light and friendly, hoping Frank would get the message and offer to change his ways, but he was oblivious. Chris knew he would have to lead the discussion.

DECODE – what's the cause?

MARY

Mary values harmony and good working relationships. She doesn't like conflict and feels uncomfortable when people argue or there is tension in the group. She prefers not to rock the boat for fear of upsetting people. She believes that happy workers are productive workers and that people will always do the right thing when you give them a chance.

Mary can often be heard saying things like, "That's okay. Let's just see how it goes." She will basically say anything to keep things civil. Mary's intention is to keep the peace and protect the relationships she has with others.

Mary's reluctance to engage in any conflict means that she appears to have double standards as she will quickly give in to anyone who pushes back. She is also training her team to believe that they can get away with whatever they want if they create friction. Peers find it difficult to trust her, as they are never sure whether she is on board or appearing to go with the flow to avoid conflict.

CHRIS

Chris knows Mary is good with people. Her team feels that she has their back and she cares. However without the ability to this with some tough love, team performance is dropping. Chris has also noticed team members pushing the boundaries of what was 'acceptable' as Mary refuses to tackle the issues. She is developing a reputation for being a 'pushover' and people are taking advantage of this. This reputation has even extended to her customers and Chris has noticed her contracts with clients generally have the largest discounts available. Her accounts are making insufficient margin as she continues to cave in to her client's negotiation tactics.

Chris has also noticed that the quality of her team's work is dropping, as there are no consequences for poor performance.

TEAM

Mary's team regards her as a 'soft touch'. Because she is so nice, she rarely calls them out when their work is not up to scratch. Some love this as it allows them to cruise along in their roles while others are frustrated by the lack of accountability this creates amongst the group. When Mary tries to assert her authority everyone knows that she won't reinforce what she's said and that there won't be any consequences for not following her requests. Mary just lets things slide. This has caused some team members to lose respect for her and others to go above her to get things handled 'properly'.

Some team members are also unsure about whether they will develop in their roles as Mary is uncomfortable giving them critical or constructive feedback, even when they ask for it. She just reinforces the things they are doing well which leaves them without clear direction for development.

SOME POSSIBLE CAUSES

Fear of not being liked

Constructive conflict requires emotional resilience. Conflict creates a perceived risk of broken social bonds, and yet is a necessary part of working with others. However, avoiding the potential of this is as useful as carrying an umbrella every single day in case of rain. It's an overreaction. A leader needs to cultivate the emotional resilience to maintain relationships while having critical conversations.

When a leader avoids conflict, they run the risk of pushing the conflict underground or causing the unaddressed situation to escalate. This can cause a loss of integrity, and also robs both parties of the opportunity to constructively resolve the situation and gain new insights.

Clumsy critical conversationalist

Constructive conflict requires skill. It requires tact, empathy, diplomacy and integrity. Without practice or a clear process to follow, leaders are at risk of responding emotionally and instinctively without preparation or due consideration.

This can adversely affect the value of addressing the situation in the first place, as clumsy communication can make the situation worse.

Fear of strong emotional responses

Conflict can cause heightened emotional states. People are unpredictable at the best of times and when under threat, their range and scale of responses can be vast. Being willing to face potential negative reactions is a necessary part of finding the courage to engage in meaningful dialogue.

An inability to be comfortable in the space of strong emotions can cause leaders to avoid situations where the other person's reactions are anticipated to be overly emotional. Some may also fear the situation will escalate unnecessarily, or that the situation will be used against them.

Burying their head in the sand

Conflict rarely goes away on its own. Dealing with conflict requires the strength of conviction that addressing the situation is worth the potential risk.

A leader who avoids confrontation in the hope that it will just go away runs the risk of making the situation worse over time.

DESIGN – what's the action?

SNAPSHOT OF CURRENT THINKING

Peter Senge in *The Fifth Discipline* wrote, "Contrary to popular myth, great teams are not characterized by an absence of conflict. On the contrary, in my experience, one of the most reliable indicators of a team that is continually learning is the visible conflict of ideas. In great teams conflict becomes productive."[55]

If conflict can produce such positive outcomes, why do many leaders shy away from it? First and foremost, at the primitive level, our brain is hardwired to avoid conflict. The brain perceives a threat five times faster than a reward and as George Kohlrieser states in his book, *Hostage at the Table: How Leaders can Overcome Conflict, Influence Others, and Raise Performance*, "The mind's eye tells us, 'Conflict could be dangerous'."[56]

Consistent with the view of Senge above, Kohlrieser states that "conflict must be seen as a challenge, a problem to be solved, an opportunity, and, in that sense, something positive."[57] Kohlrieser, an internationally recognised expert in leadership, draws upon his experience as a veteran hostage negotiator to explain how the techniques and psychological insights used in hostage negotiations can have a broader application to any relationship.

Here are Kohlrieser's 10 steps[58] for successful conflict resolution:

1. **Form a bond**

   This is paramount and means more than talking; it involves the creation of an emotional synergy. This does not mean that you have to like them, but is "an exchange of energy that keeps people engaged in a way that holds the relationship together in difficult moments."[59]

2. **Separate the person from the problem**

   Self-evident, and a major challenge for many people. The person is not the problem. When you label someone, you de-personalise them and risk destroying the bond and breaching point 1 above.

3. **Identify needs, wants and interests of self**

   Understand what you want from the negotiation as well as what you don't want, otherwise you risk getting 'lost' in the negotiation. It helps to provide a foundation to move out from.

4. **Identify needs, wants and interests of the other person(s)**

   Show empathy through listening, as this reinforces the bond. Understanding their needs, interests and wants helps the negotiation and reinforces your focus on the problem rather than the person.

5. **Use focused dialogue**

   The dialogue assists with clarification and understanding between the sides. From this point of understanding you can bargain for mutual benefit.

6. **Creating a goal and finding common goals**

   The goal is the focus of the process at each point in the process. The first goal may be to form the bond. Once this is done, the goal is to identify the key problems to be resolved, etc. Kohlrieser emphasises that a position is not a goal, as it is a fight for territory rather than a fight for common interests.[60]

7. **Finding options, generating proposals and making concessions**
    This is simply about exploring the alternative ways you can reach a resolution.

8. **Bargaining for a mutual benefit**
    "In a successful negotiation both parties win something and both parties give up something."[61]

9. **Coming to an agreement**
    This can be formal or informal, verbal or written.

10. **Ending or continuing the relationship on a positive note**
    This allows for successful future negotiations as the negotiation ended on a positive note.

In the words of Ronald Reagan, "Peace is not the absence of conflict, it is the ability to handle conflict by peaceful means." Kohlrieser's framework puts the relationship at the centre point of the resolution of any conflict, and as such serves to facilitate a process where peaceful resolution of conflict can occur.

COACHING TIPS TO DECREASE CONFLICT AVERSION

Minimise the fear of not being liked

- Where else has a fear of not being liked held you back? Is this a pattern? See this situation as an opportunity to break that pattern.

- What's the cost of worrying about not being liked?

- When has putting someone else's needs ahead of your own become a problem for you?

- How would you handle the situation if you knew it would turn out ok? Try this and see what happens.

- When have you faced a hard conversation and still had a good outcome? Why did it work out? How can you replicate that?

- What do you need to believe to let go of the fear of not being liked?

Build critical conversation skills

- Who do you know who has great critical conversation skills? How can you learn from them?

- Identify someone in your workplace who has these skills. Ask them to observe you at work and give you targeted feedback to improve your performance.

- Prior to conducting any planned critical conversation, find a trusted colleague and role-play the discussion first.

- Find a process that will help you handle conflict situations with greater diplomacy. Practise the process on others to safely build these new skills.

Fear of strong emotional responses

- Imagine that the strength of the other person's reaction is equal to the depth of their underlying fear or uncertainty. How does this knowledge increase your empathy for them and relax your fear of their response?

- Act as if the stronger the negative response the quicker the conflict will be addressed. How can this encourage you to allow the emotional responses to occur?

- If handling strong emotions of others was a rite of passage for true leadership, how would that change your response to these situations?

- What meaning are you making of the strong emotional response of others? What other meanings are possible and how might those shift your response to the situation?

Burying their head in the sand

- Where has ignoring conflict caught you out in the past? What was the impact of the increased time between the conflict arising and the conflict resolving?

- What would someone who handles conflict courageously and quickly tell you to do right now?

- If the potential of a bad result increases with the amount of time it takes you to confront the situation, how long are you prepared to leave a conflict unaddressed? What's the real cost to others of doing this?

- How might ignoring the situation be impacting your reputation?

- What might others start doing as a result of your reluctance to address the situation?

SUMMARY

- Issues are not addressed.

- The prevailing perception is she's a soft touch.

- The direct report's driving intention is to maintain harmony and good working relationships.

- Possible drivers? They may fear not being liked; they lack the skills for critical conversations; they fear strong emotional responses; they bury their head in the sand.

Fence-sitter
indecisive leader

"Nothing is more difficult, and therefore more precious, than to be able to decide."
Napoleon Bonaparte

A bad decision is often better than no decision at all. Stalling decisions creates bottlenecks and blockages. Action precedes clarity, so make a decision and take action.

She says

What do other people think?

She thinks

Making good decisions is important.
Need to gather all valid ideas and data.
Everyone has a voice.
Building consensus creates ownership.

He thinks

There are too many meetings.
Her decisions take time.
She seems uncertain or lacking confidence.
She doesn't back herself with peers.
She is easily persuaded by others.

Her intention

Get the right outcome.

360 feedback

- Mary is always asking me what I think or what we should decide. 'We' shouldn't decide, 'she' should decide. I'm not the leader – she is.

- Mary builds a great team environment but sometimes I feel we are going around in circles. I think she needs to make quicker decisions so we can move forward.

- Meetings run by Mary are painful. They take sooo long and nothing is ever decided. It was a mistake to put her in charge.

- Mary can't make a decision to save herself. It's annoying.

- She calls her style 'collaborative'. We call it 'death by meeting'.

DISCOVER – what's the problem?

Before Mary's promotion she was a star in the department. However since being put in charge of the logistics department and therefore responsible for a team of people, a departmental budget and strategic initiatives, her performance has declined and so too has the department. After careful observation, Chris finally worked out why – a lack of decision-making.

Mary spent too long making decisions – if she even made them at all. Sometimes she would consult way too broadly, and at other times she would sit on a decision and try to buy more time if she was pushed for an answer. This behaviour was crippling her department. Chris thought back to the numerous requests he had from other stakeholders in his inbox to 'push things through' and 'get things moving' because of Mary's failure to make decisions. Her actions were causing bottlenecks on key projects and people had started coming to him for a decision.

Chris knew Mary had the skills and knowledge to run the team. He also knew that something needed to be done about this problem and quickly.

DECODE – what's the cause?

MARY

Mary values great results. Making good decisions is an important part of doing a good job. Mary strives to make good decisions by getting as much information as possible, or consulting with all the right parties, or sometimes just letting the passage of time reveal the right decision. She does whatever it takes to ensure a good outcome.

Mary can often be heard saying things like, "What do other people think?" and "Let's just wait and see".

Mary's intention is to get the right outcome by making strong, robust decisions, and yet the unintended consequence of her approach is producing the exact opposite. Her decisions are too slow, overly consultative and do more harm than good for the progress of the department. Her team is also questioning whether she should be in the new role.

CHRIS

Chris is confident that Mary knows what she's doing and is dedicated to doing a great job. That's why he promoted her. He is also concerned that this desire to do well has crippled her ability to make decisions and lead her team effectively. Her team is questioning her ability as they interpret her ineffective decision-making strategies as a lack of knowing or lack of confidence. Stakeholders have questioned Chris's decision to put her in the role and have started to bypass her wherever possible.

Mary's desire to get it right is backfiring and ironically she is in danger of losing her position, as the department can't carry the weight of this issue for much longer. Chris is disappointed and wants to avoid this outcome.

TEAM

Mary's team is frustrated. When she first became their leader, the group agreed that she was such a breath of fresh air compared to their last leader. She actually cared about what they thought and asked for their input into important decisions. Lately, they are beginning to think she doesn't know what she's doing. She asks for their input on everything, sits on decisions for too long, and her desk is buried under the piles of information she pores over before giving any answers. She is no longer a breath of fresh air!

The team wants confidence and clear direction from Mary. They want someone who is not afraid to make a call and keep things moving forward. They want leadership.

SOME POSSIBLE CAUSES

Perfectionist

Decisions are not guaranteed. Decisions are prone to be incomplete or even wrong at times, however leaders accept this as the reality of decision-making. It is unrealistic to expect the right decision every time.

Leaders who aim for perfection can stall decision-making as they attempt to cover all bases, but the opportunity may pass in the meantime.

Fear of being accountable for a poor decision

Decisions can go badly. It's a risk every leader must face. Some leaders will avoid making a decision, as they do not want to be held accountable if things go wrong. Yet not making a decision for fear of the wrong decision, can also lead to the leader being held responsible.

Preference to share decision-making responsibility with others

Conventional wisdom says 'a problem shared is a problem halved'. Involving others in decision-making can spread the load of a difficult decision and lead to a more robust and well-thought-through result.

Socialising a decision can also increase engagement and commitment to action. Leaders who involve stakeholders in decisions may get things done more quickly over the long term, even if it takes more time up front.

When taken to the extreme however, this decision-making style can create inefficiencies. Leaders who rely on external input for all decisions, large and small, run the risk of creating a bottleneck and appearing as if they don't know what to do. This can affect the trust people are willing to place in the leader and is likely to impact the leader's authority.

Lack of clarity on values or outcome

Decision-making is an art that requires a choice between competing elements. When leaders have strong values and clear goals, decision-making is easier. They know what's most important about the decision and they know what they want as a result of the decision.

When leaders are not sure what's important to them, and/or are unclear on the objectives, making decisions can feel like an impossible task, and this leader may appear indecisive to others.

Too many decisions to make

Decision-making requires cognitive effort. Every decision made reduces the pool of resources available to make future decisions. This resource is finite and can be exhausted at varying speeds. Leaders who understand this pace themselves and factor this into their decision-making day.

When leaders feel overloaded by too many decisions, they can suffer from decision fatigue and could appear to be unable to make what may be quite a simple decision.

DESIGN – what's the action?

SNAPSHOT OF CURRENT THINKING

"When it comes to making decisions, it's clear that our brains are flawed instruments."[62] *Chip and Dan Heath, authors of the bestselling book, Decisive.*

Leaders need to be aware of the impact of not making decisions. It is a leader's role to make decisions and this role should not be deferred, deflected or abdicated to anyone else or to time.

Dr Hossein Arshan is a research professor at the University of Baltimore and Teaching Professor at the Johns Hopkins Carey Business School. In his publication *Leadership Decision Making*, he lists characteristics of 'good' decision makers as:[63]

- having a high tolerance for ambiguity
- having a well-ordered sense of priorities

- being a good listener
- always building the consensus around a decision
- avoiding stereotypes
- remaining resilient with feedback
- being comfortable with both soft and hard input
- being realistic about cost and difficulty
- avoiding a decision minefield

Even knowing how to make good decisions may not be enough. We are all at risk of 'decision fatigue' if we are forced to make too many decisions. In a research study[64] published by the National Academy of Sciences, psychologists examined the factors that impact whether or not a judge approves a criminal for parole. They analysed more than 1,100 decisions by a parole board and found this startling statistic: "Prisoners who appeared early in the morning received parole about 70 per cent of the time, while those who appeared late in the day were paroled less than 10 per cent of the time." While it could be thought that this was a factor of the judge's judicial discretion, in fact this was not the case. The judge's rulings were impacted by all types of things that should be irrelevant in the courtroom including the time of day and timing of breaks.

This is a clear example of decision fatigue. The cognitive load of making another decision towards the end of the day resulted in them making the 'no parole' decision – the default decision easiest to make. If unaware, leaders are also at risk of decision fatigue influencing their ability to make quality decisions.

COACHING TIPS TO INCREASE DECISIVENESS

Release the need for perfection

- How much time are you spending trying to get things perfect? What could you do instead if you weren't doing that?

- Consider the 80/20 rule. Eighty per cent of your impact will come from 20 per cent of your effort. What can you let go of because it probably doesn't matter?

- Consider someone around you whose work you respect and who sometimes gets things wrong. What can you learn from them?

- What's the worst that can happen if the decision isn't perfect?

- Life as we know it will not end with an error in this decision. Act as if this were true, decide now, and move on.

- Each day this week, practise making small decisions with little thought. Notice what this frees up for you.

Step up and be accountable

- What if the risk of this decision was increased by your delay? Make a decision right now and carry on.

- Act as if you believed that making some poor decisions was an acceptable occupational hazard for a leader. Believing this, what would you decide right now?

- There are no mistakes, only learning. How can the lessons from a poor decision inform your decision-making for next time?

- What are you modelling for your team by your apparent reluctance to take responsibility? What would you prefer to be demonstrating?

- Remember when someone you respect made a poor decision.

- Fear of what others think (FoWOT) can be a debilitating disease for leaders. Imagine you just swallowed the FoWOT-antidote pill. What would you do next?

- What would you do if you weren't afraid? Do more of that and build up your fear immunity.

Make independent decisions

- One helpful delusion is that you will only ever face decisions you are equipped to handle. What would enable that belief right now?

- Stop asking questions and take action now based on what you know.

- What if your desire for collaboration was seen by others as an inability to decide? What would you do differently?

- Draw on your own knowledge, trust your inner voice and back yourself.

- Ask yourself what your mentor would do in this situation, and do it.

- In this decision, trust yourself and just decide. Review the outcome to learn for next time.

- Imagine you are giving someone else advice on how to make this decision. Take your own advice.

- Where might your need for constant collaboration be limiting the empowerment of your team?

Get clear on your values and outcome

- Consult a reference on decision-making to understand some key decision-making frameworks. One such book is *Decisive*[65] by Chip and Dan Heath.

- What is really important to you in making this decision? Use this knowledge to provide a framework for deciding.

- List the most important criteria for this decision. What are your non-negotiables?

- What are your must-haves for this outcome? What decision needs to be made to ensure you achieve these?

- Imagine this decision was already made? What was the criteria on which you made it?

- What are you willing to compromise on? What will you not compromise on? How does this inform your decision-making?

- How will this decision demonstrate your values to others? Make that decision.

Manage decision fatigue

- Make your most important and/or most challenging decisions when you are fresh.

- Delegate authority for small and unimportant decisions to your team and save your cognitive resource for significant decisions.

- Notice when you are struggling to make a decision. Walk away and clear your head before re-engaging.

- Make less important or challenging decisions later in the day.

- Map your energy levels during the day and use this knowledge to plan when to address big decisions.

- How can you tell the difference between decision fatigue and that you are facing a tough decision?

- How can you build awareness of the difference between an inability to make a decision due to decision fatigue, as opposed to just struggling with a genuinely difficult decision? Use this awareness to build appropriate strategies.

SUMMARY

- Progress stalls.
- The prevailing perception is a lack of confidence to make a decision.
- The direct report's driving intention is achieving great results.
- Possible drivers? They may be a perfectionist; they fear being accountable for a poor decision; they care about team input; they lack clarity on values or outcomes; they have too many decisions to make.

Know-it-all
closed to other ideas

**"Men cease to think when
they think they know it all."**
Horace

Knowing it all means there's nothing more to learn and no professional
growth. Closing your mind to new ideas will mean you are left behind.
Ignorance of your ignorance can be catastrophic. Seek feedback from
others and be open to new ideas to keep your leadership developing.

She says

I just know.

She thinks

I know the best way to handle this.
I don't care what they think.
I need to stay ahead of the game.
I've been doing this a long time.

He thinks

It's impossible to coach her.
People work with her under sufferance.
There's a 'cost' to team dynamics.
She's fixed in views.
She only engages when she agrees.

Her intention

Back her strengths and deliver quality.

360 feedback

- Mary is not open to new ideas.

- She's not listening to any of our suggestions.

- She's a bit of a know-it-all. She has an opinion on everything.

- She's argumentative. She's always disagreeing with what I say. I know she's very clever but sometimes it's just too much.

- I don't bother offering any suggestions any more – there's no point.

- I cringe at the way she sometimes argues with our customers.

DISCOVER – what's the problem?

Chris hired a coach to work with Mary after receiving one too many complaints about how difficult she was to work with. The coach was now in Chris's office, expressing her concern that Mary may prove to be uncoachable. The coach was reluctant to take Mary on as she appeared fixed in her views and reluctant to consider perspectives other than her own, despite some clear feedback that this style was not working for the rest of her team. Mary dismissed the feedback, expressing the opinion that, "they don't really know what I do".

Chris recognised this as Mary's pattern. Not taking feedback, not involving others in decisions or asking for input, or asking for input only to disregard the advice and doing what she wanted to in the first place. Mary was not open to the ideas of her team and seemed to back herself exclusively. Her leadership style was causing morale issues in her team and the regional office staff was reluctant to deal with her. Chris had even overheard her on the phone arguing with a customer about the opinions he was expressing and insisting he was wrong. Chris had also noticed that Mary would only comply with his requests when she agreed with them. Most other times she took his directions as suggestions, which she often ignored. He worried about how to resolve the situation if this coach refused to take Mary on.

DECODE – what's the cause?

MARY

Mary values holding true to her ideas and decisions. She backs her own judgment and is able to decide for herself without needing outside help or opinions. Her strong internal sense of knowing allows her to make decisions quickly and easily.

She is often heard saying things like, "I just know", "I've been doing this a long time" and "I don't care what they think".

Mary's intention is to back her strengths to deliver quality results.

The unintended consequence of deciding for herself is that she often puts people offside when she dismisses their ideas and input. This limits her ability to influence and engage others in the work. She is also gaining a reputation as being arrogant, overly confident and not capitalising on the strengths of others nor the diversity of ideas in her team. She is increasingly being viewed as impossible to work with.

CHRIS

Chris has experienced both the upside and the downside of Mary's tendency to make her own decisions without involving others. This preference has been useful when Mary was operating in an environment where there were no precedents and lots of new decisions to be made every day. However, as soon as Mary needed to build consensus and get buy-in from others, this style became her downfall. Without the motivation to take on board ideas and suggestions from others, Mary becomes closed to new ideas. She remains fixed in her views and is hard to persuade that alternatives should even be considered. Her key stakeholders are not behind her as most feel irrelevant and dismissed.

TEAM

Mary's team experience her as arrogant and dismissive. They feel she only ever engages with their ideas when she agrees with them. Some members of the team appreciate her level of confidence, however, most find her exhausting. They wonder why they are even needed as their input is so rarely considered.

SOME POSSIBLE CAUSES

Self-referencing

Leading a team requires engagement. With engagement comes ownership of the work, discretionary effort and better outcomes. Leaders who struggle to include the opinions of others, and are reluctant to seek advice or input from others, are in danger of losing the valuable contribution and results that comes from an engaged workforce.

Over-confidence

Confidence is an important leadership trait. Confidence inspires others to believe that the chosen path will deliver results. Over-confidence can blind leaders, limiting their motivation and ability to draw on the full range of skills, resources and opinions available to them. Over-confidence is an emotional feeling that often leads to an increased amount of self-referencing. (Note, sometimes a display of over-confidence may actually be protecting low self-esteem.)

DESIGN – what's the action?

SNAPSHOT OF CURRENT THINKING

The only true wisdom is in knowing you know nothing.
Socrates

We are in the era of the knowledge worker and, in the past, knowledge meant power. This has led to some leaders over-emphasising the value of their individual knowledge. However our world is also rapidly changing and therefore the ability to take on new knowledge and adapt has become paramount if a leader is to successfully lead their organisation in a sustainable way.

A know-it-all is often highly defensive and may invalidate new information, or an idea that is not their own, on the basis that their knowledge is superior. They will often point out the failures of ideas where they believe issues could have been avoided if people had listened to them. If left unchecked, a know-it-all manager can impact their team's morale and cause resentment in their co-workers.

In his book *Thinking Fast and Slow*[66], Nobel Prize winner and behavioural economist, Daniel Kahneman provides an explanation of the systems in the brain that govern how we filter information and their potential impacts upon our judgment and decision-making. These systems are known as System 1 and System 2. System 1 runs automatically and quickly with little or no effort or voluntary control. System 2 allocates attention to the effortful mental activities that demand it, and is often associated with choice and concentration.

System 1 thinking is the cognitive playground and safe zone of the know-it-all. System 1 thinking relies heavily on our existing model of the world. It drives our learned emotional responses to stimuli, creating endless shortcuts in our thinking known as heuristics. These models are based on our background, education, experience, assumptions and beliefs, which may or may not be true. To foster efficiency, System 1 seeks out ways to validate and confirm information to align with our existing beliefs. It can also alter how the information is interpreted or prioritised; a phenomenon known by scientists as confirmation bias.

While valuable for intuitive or repetitive tasks, System 1 thinking can lead to us blocking out information that challenges our existing view. Known as cognitive dissonance, our ego-defence system kicks into play, leading us to rationalise the information to make it fit with what is already known. We are essentially cognitively blind to different ideas or interpretations.

To overcome System 1 thinking requires effort from System 2. This is hard work and so we have a natural preference for System 1 thinking. As Kahneman states, "It is easier to recognise other people's mistakes [in thinking] than our own."[67] We need to overcome our natural tendency to reject ideas that don't fit with our current thinking. Described by Jack Mezirow[68] as 'transformative learning', this requires effortful reflection and evaluation of current assumptions.

Edward Hess, author of *Learn or Die* states that learning involves a diverse set of cognitive operations and we develop efficient and effective learning skills through practice, practice and more practice.[69] He describes the process of adult learning as a "process of modifying or completely changing our mental models based on new experiences or evidence" and we need to be open-minded to do this. Hess names four other relevant biases that are important for learning and are often evident in the approach of the know-it-all:

1. **Availability bias** which causes us to reach for the easiest option i.e. information that is available but may be wrong.

2. **Self-interest bias** that influences us to make self-serving decisions even in the face of conflicting data.

3. **Anchoring bias** which prevents the exploration of options because we are chained to a particular piece of data.

4. **Superiority illusion** or, "I made the decision so it must be a good one". This means the person has now become emotionally invested in the decision and will defend it.

Adaptive leadership is the antidote for the know-it-all. (See page 237 of this book for more information). Adaptive leadership requires the leader to commit to the process of learning, unlearning and re-learning on an ongoing basis. (See page 27 for a more detailed explanation of this process).

COACHING TIPS TO ENCOURAGE OPENNESS TO OTHER IDEAS

Genuinely involve others in decision-making

- How could your performance be improved by consulting others and allowing their input to be right?

- What do you need to believe in order to allow others to change your opinion?

- What is your typical response when other people offer you suggestions? How might this be impacting their motivation to keep providing input in future?

- How do you positively reinforce contribution of new ideas from others? What other ways could be possible?

- In your next meeting, note how many ideas are offered and use this as a benchmark as you build your ability to welcome and utlise the input of others.

- Assume the client has critical input. Check in with them and dig deeper for a richer result.

- Act as if all feedback were true, and try it on before discarding it.

- Ask three colleagues for feedback on your performance in relation to genuinely involving others in decision-making. Consider how you might work differently as a result.

- Appearing to ignore the input of others creates disengagement. How does a lack of team engagement impact your overall outcomes?

Develop an appropriate level of confidence

- What perspectives or new ideas could become available to you if you acted as if you were wrong right now? What actions might you take?

- What if, as the leader, your high level of confidence was suppressing great ideas within the group? Act as if this were true for a week and sit on your opinions to see what changes in the group dynamic.

- Remember a time when your opinion was neither sought nor valued at work. How did that impact your engagement levels and affect the quality of the outcome? How might you be inadvertently doing that to your team right now?

- At the end of your client meetings, ask your colleagues to rate the quality of your option exploration with the client, before closing down to a confident decision.

- At your next meeting, record the ratio of questions to statements directed at the other attendee(s). What does this tell you about how your high levels of confidence might appear to others as arrogance or inflexibility?

- How can you channel and utilise the state of uncertainty as a natural moderator of overconfidence? How could this create more space for others to contribute?

SUMMARY

- New ideas are stifled.
- The prevailing perception is being closed to other ideas.
- The direct report's driving intention is to back themselves.
- Possible drivers? They may prefer to back their own judgment, or are over-confident.

Guardian
inability to innovate

"Innovation is anything, but business as usual."
Anonymous

Yesterday's genius is tomorrow's old news. The environment is changing so quickly that if you're not moving ahead you're falling behind. Maintaining the status quo is not enough. New ideas and taking calculated risks keeps you in the game.

She says

This is the way we have always done it.

She thinks

Let's stick with what we know.
No point in change for change's sake.
We know this way works.

He thinks

She doesn't cope well with the unexpected.
Thinking laterally is not her strong point –
she lacks innovation.
She needs a high level of certainty to proceed.

Her intention

Guaranteeing consistent quality results.

360 feedback

- She is 'old school'.

- I feel like Mary is really behind the times.

- She is resistant to good ideas.

- It's sometimes great and sometimes frustrating to work with Mary. It's great because she really knows her stuff and it's frustrating because she won't allow me to try anything new.

- Mary is great with her customers.

- She is very protective of the status quo and is afraid to upset the apple cart by introducing new processes even when we know the changes will improve our workflow.

DISCOVER – what's the problem?

All the team was on board with the new product launch, except for Mary … again. She didn't see the point in developing a new product suite. Her clients were perfectly happy with the current products. It was hard to argue with her as her account had some of the highest results in terms of customer satisfaction and loyalty across the region, however Chris was still worried. Every time new ideas or innovations were discussed Mary would defend the status quo. She appeared stuck in her thinking and too wedded to the current activity to see the writing on the wall.

Chris had seen this before. He knew that if his team wasn't moving forward in terms of new products, new ideas and new market opportunities, they were actually going backwards. Mary's reluctance to innovate and try new things to grow the accounts impeded her ability to adapt quickly to new changes and shifting landscapes and ultimately, the market would move forward without her.

DECODE – what's the cause?

MARY

Mary values a stable working environment with clear and known parameters. She has built a strong skills base and a solid reputation in the current environment and is proud of the good work she does. Results are strong and nothing is broken. She finds the CEO's focus on change and the expectation to try new things exhausting. The old ways work fine. Why change for change's sake and just create more work for everyone if it fails?

She's often heard saying things like, "This is the way we've always done it because it works every time."

Mary's intention is to guarantee consistent quality results.

The unintended consequences of doing what she's always done and not thinking outside the box is that high change environments are stressful for Mary. Being required to keep pace with constant change and adapt accordingly is overwhelming. As a result Mary gravitates towards roles and projects that are 'stable' but not 'sexy' or progressive. She secretly fears her skills are becoming redundant and works to promote the benefits of the status quo.

CHRIS

Chris appreciates the depth of knowledge, experience and expertise that Mary brings to the team. He's worried that she's stifling the good ideas of her team and also very aware that her portfolio is not growing at the rate of other account directors, despite showing strong customer satisfaction.

The business environment is evolving, demanding alternative strategies and new ways of interacting with customers. Mary shows obvious discomfort with, and resistance to, the new or unexpected. Last week, she missed a big opportunity to expand the current contract with an existing client because she missed the cues for a new opportunity. Her inability to innovate is costing the company.

TEAM

Mary's team experience her as inflexible and unwilling to try new ideas. They are frustrated with lack of creativity and wish she would take more risks and 'get with the program'. They think she gets easily overwhelmed when having to adapt her way of working, and therefore most have stopped offering new ideas. Some spend more time on Facebook.

They respect her knowledge but feel she is 'stuck in her ways' and will never support anything she sees as risky – and she sees most things as risky. They find it hard to try new things and develop new skills under her leadership because the risk of failure is not an option for Mary.

SOME POSSIBLE CAUSES

Too busy to think creatively

Innovation is a process that can be learnt and employed. New insights and understanding often emerge when the brain switches off its active focus on a particular topic. After thoroughly immersing yourself in the topic, 'walking away' or taking a break from the effort will often give rise to new insights and new ideas.

If people are stretched so thinly at work that they don't have time to pause or let their mind wander (to do the real innovation work!), the conditions for innovation are stifled. With a lack of new ideas flowing, people may be under pressure to 'think harder' which goes completely against the creative process. Paradoxically, generating new ideas is not just about more effort. It's also about allowing the space for good ideas to arise.

Risk averse

Innovation requires risk taking. Ideas need to be trialled and tested and good innovators know to expect a decent amount of failure along the way. It's par for the course.

When an organisation wants more innovation from its leaders, but when the culture (or the style of individual leaders) does not tolerate failure, people receive mixed messages about what is more important – new ideas or getting things right. People may become too scared to innovate for fear of an adverse reaction.

Fear of change

Innovation requires change. Change by its very nature is ambiguous and ambiguity generates a threat response in the brain. For some leaders, this pushes them so far outside their comfort zone that their performance declines and the security of the familiar is sought.

While a leader who focuses on maintaining the status quo and enjoys stable and routine working environments may build deep knowledge banks in their particular fields, they can also struggle to keep up with the changing environment.

Overly procedural

Innovation requires the ability to consider possible alternatives. Possibilities and options are the pathway to innovation, allowing a movement from linear to lateral thinking and making connections between the seemingly unconnected.

A leader who is focused on doing things procedurally because they can rely on replicable results takes comfort in their ability to do things the 'right way'. Others could see this leader as valuing the process more than the outcome.

DESIGN – what's the action?

SNAPSHOT OF CURRENT THINKING

According to the *Reference for Business: Encyclopaedia of Business (2nd ed.)*[70] people with the following behaviours and motivations are more likely to promote and advance innovation within organisations:

- Value freedom
- Take risks
- Support ideas
- Have the time to generate ideas
- Have the freedom to debate and challenge
- Feel trusted

In addition to this, Dyer et al[71] conducted research into how and when successful entrepreneurs came up with their ideas. They studied the habits of 25 innovative entrepreneurs and surveyed more than 3,000 executives and 500 individuals who had started innovative companies or invented new products, over a six-year period. They came up with five key 'discovery skills' that underpinned the behaviours of disruptive innovators: *associational thinking (drawing links between unrelated fields), questioning, observing, experimenting and networking.* Innovators made one or more of these a daily event.

They found that "innovative entrepreneurs (who are also CEOs) spend 50% more time on these discovery activities than do CEOs with no track record for innovation." Most importantly, they also concluded that these skills did not have to be innate, they could be cultivated.

Sometimes when people speak about an innovator they are thinking about an innovative leader like Steve Jobs (former CEO of Apple) or Richard Branson (Virgin). So how is an innovative leader different from an innovator? Innovative leaders "are creative visionaries who have big ideas and, most importantly, can motivate people around them to turn those ideas into reality."[72]

COACHING TIPS TO INCREASE INNOVATION

Create time for innovation

- Just like any other work activity, schedule time for reflection. Build time for reflection every day for three weeks. At the end, assess the impact this has had on your creativity.

- Start projects earlier to allow for more processing and reflection time, information gathering, idea canvassing and discussion.

- When you are stuck, take a break, go for a short walk, or do something unrelated to switch your focus. Come back refreshed and notice there's a new way to approach.

Embrace failure

- What's the worst that could happen if you failed?

- What's the upside of failure? How does it support progress?

- Who do you need support from to make failure an acceptable option for you?

- How can you demonstrate that failure is okay for the rest of your team?

- 'Fail forward' is the idea that as you fail something you learn something else to maximise your success next time. Pretend for a week you believe in 'fail forward' and notice the freedom this gives you to be more innovative.

- What negative associations do you have with failure? How can you challenge these beliefs to support you rather than restrict you?

- Where in the past have you 'failed' at something and that has turned out to be a good thing?

- What if the maxim 'there's no failure – only learning' were true for you? What would you do now?

- What do you need to believe about risks to encourage you to take more of them?

- How can you experiment before making a decision?

- How can you run multiple tests to get more feedback and information?

Embrace change

- Imagine all the things in your world that would not have been possible if innovation and change had not occurred. What are you denying yourself, your team and the organisation by not innovating?

- Remember a time when you resisted a change that turned out to be of great benefit to you. What would that resistance have cost you? What could a reluctance to change the status quo be costing you now?

- There are ups and downs in every change. How could focusing on the downs keep you from moving forward? How could this impact your reputation and results?

- Who can you engage to support, discuss and debate your ideas?
- When faced with a familiar way of doing things, ask yourself: "Why do we do it this way? What if ...? How else ...? Why not ...?"
- Push through the status quo by imagining ridiculous scenarios that stimulate new perspectives. "How would we make money if we couldn't sell to our existing clients?" "What if no one came to work this week?"
- Interview someone who is a great innovative leader. How do they respond to change?
- What would you need to be certain of in order to welcome change? What could you do to create that sense of certainty and then embrace change?
- If you have a preference for maintaining the status quo, others may perceive you as stagnant in your perspective, or even as a blocker to change. Imagine your task today was to shatter this perception. What would you do differently?

Open up to possibilities

- Attend conferences; watch TED talks; listen to podcasts; go to live theatre shows to increase your exposure to new ideas and ways of thinking.
- Host a lunch to canvass new ideas and perspectives from an eclectic range of people.
- Propose an idea and get feedback from at least five people. Notice the power of the contributions to improving or clarifying your thinking.
- When you think you know the best way, identify just one more possibility.
- Every day this week, identify one small rule you could break in order to explore other possibilities.

- Consider the task you are about to start. Brainstorm with a change-comfortable colleague 10 different approaches you could take to achieve the same outcome.

- Consider a process that isn't working well now. Develop some suggestions for innovative new ways to address this issue and promote your ideas to your colleagues.

- Try travelling to work via a different route every day this week. Consider what you learnt through breaking away from your usual routine.

- Have your lunch in a different place; talk to someone outside your usual circle; sit in a different place, in order to gain new perspectives.

- Write out five questions each day on how to challenge the existing ways of operating.

SUMMARY

- Progress is prevented.

- The prevailing perception is protecting the status quo.

- The direct report's driving intention is to produce reliable outcomes.

- Possible drivers? They may be risk averse; may fear change or like the certainty of procedures and 'the way we've always done it'.

Micromanager
management on a leash

"When the boss is away, work becomes a holiday."
Portuguese proverb

Micromanagement suffocates. Paradoxically, too much care increases the manager's workload and stress, and diminishes the productivity of the team. Allowing autonomy increases engagement and frees up management capacity.

She says

Things are under review.

She thinks

If I want it done now, I have to do it myself.
I need to be sure this is right.
People need constant feedback.
Due diligence is important.

He thinks

The team's productivity is reduced.
Absenteeism is rising.
People are feeling suffocated.
She's not developing her team.

Her intention

Raise the standard through quality output.

360 feedback

- She assigns us work and then constantly interferes.

- My seven-year-old gets more scope to choose the way he works than we do here!

- Returning work back with red scribbles all over it (again!) is not the way to motivate a professional team.

- Working with Mary is like working in a cartoon about micromanagement!

- She doesn't trust anyone but herself.

- She has no idea of the skills of her team or how to use them.

- Time for me to find somewhere else where I can stretch myself.

- She over-engineers things and then insists that I follow the process she has developed.

- I think she means well but her need to be 'diligent' is blocking our progress.

DISCOVER – what's the problem?

Chris knew his wife wouldn't be happy – the networking function with the board had gone much longer than he expected and he was very late leaving. He walked past Mary's office not surprised to see her bent over her desk.

Mary was looking so tired recently, and seemed to be very bogged down in the work of the department. She had a team of young and keen marketers. Each one had a strong resumé and good track record, and yet she didn't seem able to trust them to do their work without supervision.

As he drove home, Chris realised that since Mary had taken over, the whole team seemed to have lost the energy and buzz he had come to expect from the marketing department. Mary seemed overwhelmed and the team seemed to be rapidly losing motivation. He was also starting to get complaints from other departments waiting on outstanding work and unable move forward without Mary's contribution.

DECODE – what's the cause?

MARY

Producing a quality outcome is very important to Mary. She focuses on maintaining control of the work to ensure that the desired standard is reached. Despite providing clear instructions on how things need to be done, she often finds that to guarantee good work she needs to provide constant feedback and check all outputs at least twice.

Mary has heard some of the team say she is a micromanager, but she shrugs that off. After all, she doesn't want to be working so late! It's just the price she has to pay to make sure the job is done well. She is becoming frustrated because it seems that the more specific feedbackshe gives about the required improvements, the less effort her team are putting in, and the more mistakes she is finding in their work.

Mary's intention is to raise the standard of the department by ensuring 100 per cent quality deliverables. Due diligence is important to her in ensuring a solid outcome of the highest quality. She's often heard saying that things are "under review".

The unintended consequence of her approach is lack of development in her team. Her concern for high standards is being perceived as lack of trust, and so they no longer feel empowered to make things happen. Her peers around the leadership table see her as inflexible, one even commenting on her 'paranoia'.

Mary herself is starting to feel the pressure of letting others down and is worried that she might not be doing this job as well as she had hoped. Getting this promotion was a big break for her and she desperately wants to do well. She wonders if maybe she just needs to work harder?

CHRIS

Chris knows that Mary means well, and in other roles her constant need to thoroughly check the work of others would be an asset. It's just not an asset for the Director of Marketing! Right now her micromanagement was impacting on Chris through Mary's reduction in productivity from the marketing department. This was costing Mary personally, and seemed to be having a serious impact on the morale of the marketing team. He had even noticed that for the first time ever, marketing showed on the monthly absentee report.

Chris was beginning to question his decision to move Mary into this role. She had been such an excellent marketing analyst, and yet Chris knew the CEO was beginning to doubt Mary's ability to shine in this role.

TEAM

Mary's team experience her as a 'micromanager' at best, and a 'control freak' at worst, reporting that she allocates work and then interferes with getting it done. Some more flexible members of the team initially gave her the benefit of doubt, thinking she would relax a bit once she settled into her new role. But that hasn't happened. They perceive her as a bottleneck – because she needs to review and approve <u>all</u> work, everything is held up on Mary's desk and it has become almost impossible to meet deadlines.

People have stopped trying to defend their work and demonstrate to Mary that a different way is possible. It seems that only Mary's way can be trusted. One person in the team cheekily says he loves working with Mary because he now 'switches off' and does the minimum, knowing that Mary will take over and finish it anyway regardless of what he does!

SOME POSSIBLE CAUSES

Low trust

Trusting in the people you work with enables autonomy. Failing to trust damages relationships and ultimately the productivity of the team.

A leader with low trust may treat each circumstance as a new event and will test it as if for the first time, leading to frustration in their team. This leader may also lack trust in their own capabilities.

High detailed focus

The higher the level, the broader the focus needed. As a leader progresses up the corporate ladder, less detail and more big-picture thinking is required. A leader who is motivated to work sequentially through tasks and/or take a detailed approach can appear to be micromanaging. This leader may prefer to work from the bottom up and focus on the individual details that make up the whole.

This leader could appear to be focusing energy on things that are not strategically important, or seeking involvement in everything so they feel across the topic. This leader may also find delegation challenging, as they may feel uncomfortable letting go of the detailed knowledge.

Insistence on overly high standards

As a leader, the performance of the team matters at least as much as her own. A leader who is focused on overly high standards may take over the work of others to ensure that those high standards are maintained.

The desire for recognition of the results they have achieved may also drive micromanaging behaviours. Their high standards for themselves and others may result in them driving themselves too hard, being reluctant to delegate and suffering burn out. Their team members may even feel bullied.

Need for control

Balancing control with releasing control is a paradox of leadership. A leader who holds tightly onto control risks increasing their own anxiety while disempowering their people. A leader with an excessive need to be in charge could be viewed by others as demanding, dominating and/or directive.

A high need for control will foster micromanagement and thwart the ability to delegate due to the belief that no one can do the job as well as they do. This will often translate into high workloads and a struggle to achieve work-life balance.

Perfectionist

The quest for 'perfect' and the rejection of anything less, is a dangerous game for a leader to play. In most contexts, a leader who sets unachievable standards risks disappointment for themselves and their team. Effective leaders realise that 'failure' is a learning opportunity and perfectionism impedes progress.

The need for perfectionism can be driven by things like a fear of getting things wrong, not being good enough, or the feeling of being an imposter.

DESIGN – what's the action?

SNAPSHOT OF CURRENT THINKING

Micromanagement is readily found in organisations globally. The negative impacts on employee morale are so intense that micromanagement is among the top three reasons employees resign.[73] In a 2013 Australian Employee Engagement Survey[74], 38 per cent of professionals who responded did not agree with the statement "my manager helps me perform at my best". Tony Gleeson, Chief Executive Officer of the Australian Institute of Management Victoria and Tasmania, believes the survey result is largely due to micro managers. "Some people won't like this but I actually think micromanagement is worse for an organisation than having no management at all," he says.

Micromanagement causes employees to feel inept and creates disengagement. They fail to focus on their work, and their lack of motivation and productivity can be contagious amongst their colleagues. Micromanagement tells an employee that you don't trust their judgment or work. It is also costly, according to the book *Twelve: The Elements of Great Managing*[75], that states: "Disengagement-driven turnover costs most sizeable businesses millions every year". Contrast this with Gallup research cited in the book that finds that engaged teams average 18 per cent higher productivity and 12 per cent higher profitability than less engaged teams.

According to MindTools[76], and validated by our own experience, "Micromanagers often affirm the value of their approach with a simple experiment: They give an employee an assignment, and then disappear until the deadline." The employee is unlikely to perform well under these circumstances, especially if they have lost confidence as a result of being micromanaged until now.

The micromanager will use this result as evidence to support their view that their input is required. As observed by MindTools, "Micromanagers prevent employees from making, and taking responsibility for, their own decisions. But it's precisely the process of making decisions, and living with the consequences, that causes people to grow and improve."

COACHING TIPS TO MINIMISE MICROMANAGEMENT

Increase trust

- Giving the person the benefit of the doubt, what is the minimum amount of supervision you need to provide? Now halve this and see what happens.

- When in the past did you take too long to trust, and that lack of trust limited the development of a relationship? What did you learn that you can apply now?

- What assumptions could you make that would allow you to trust now and empower this person?

- Play the trust game both ways and share information about what you are up to, especially if it might be relevant to what your team is doing.

- Resist checking up on your team. Instead of asking whether they've finished a task, try asking questions like, "What do you need to get this project done?" or "Is anything getting in your way?"

- Rather than assuming they need your help to get it right, ask, "What do you need from me to get this done?"

- When assigning a task, establish clear milestones and delivery standards to avoid the need for regular checking. Then leave people to get the job done.

- How do you feel when you are under constant surveillance? What impact would this have on your motivation at work?

- If this saying were true: "The more you use the reins, the less they'll use their brains", how would you adjust your leadership style to use less reins?

Reduce detail focus

- What are the essential concepts you need to focus on to communicate the priorities effectively?

- How can you trust you have all the detail you need already so that you can step back, loosen the reins and allow the person to get on with the task?

- The Pareto principle states that 80 per cent of the effects come from 20 per cent of the causes. If the detail of 80 per cent of your work won't matter, what's the 20 per cent you need to focus on?

- As a person becomes more senior in an organisation, with broader responsibilities and competing demands on their time, they typically become less detailed and more big picture. What detail do you need to let go of to move from being a technician to a leader?

- Understand that you can present the overview, knowing that your audience will ask when they need more information.

- Formulate ideas in headlines and bullet points rather than sentences.

- What is the current cost to you of working continually with this level of detail? Consider the cost personally, for your team and for the organisation.

- Act as if you didn't need any of the detail, and allow your team members to know it. You know where to find them if you need them.

Choose an appropriate standard

- 100 per cent is not always required. What is the minimum standard appropriate for this situation? Manage to that standard and no more.

- What development opportunities is your team missing out on by you not sharing the work and the limelight?

- Consider the judgments you make about those who don't hold the same standards as you. Could these decisions be limiting you? What would be possible for you if you accepted they are still getting the results in spite of their standards?

- What impact could you make if you were to step back and lead from behind?

- Try out three other ways to get the work done and done well.

- How can you maintain and develop your identity as a leader while stepping back and letting others step up?

- What if you were diagnosed with an addiction to crisis, escalated stress and increased pressure? What would you do differently to address the impact of your addiction?

Relax the need for control

- Describe the impact on your current role or project if you were 20 per cent less focused on being in control and more focused on building collaboration and harmony within the team.

- What is the cost to you of putting your need for control ahead of the relationships and people connections?

- What could be freed up if you focused on establishing roles, responsibilities, accountability and expectations, and then left your team to get on with delivering to that?

- How are you hiding behind confusion and lack of role clarity? Could it be that this creates an environment for overly tight control from you?

- Approach this project with a 'beginner's mind' and explore being innocent of knowledge, taking interest in learning from what others know.

- What do you fear might happen if you to release control? Put mitigations in place and try it out.

- If you had to leave your role next week, what would be the essential things that your team would need to know from you to continue moving forward? Try providing just that level of direction and notice the job gets done anyway without so much input from you.

Banish the perfectionist

- What would you do if it were not possible for you or your team to fail? How would you lead this current project?

- How would you approach this if you believed that it was okay to fail, because failure will offer you and your team new learning to succeed next time?

- Think about a particular time when you were willing to risk failure. In your imagination, travel back through time to that place. Notice how you hold your body and how you breathe. Bring that feeling back to now and allow yourself to let go of the need for perfection in this instance.

- Imagine that everything you do is a lesson delivered to build your competency. 'Failure' is okay as it provides learning for success next time. Practise this mindset.

- Think about something you do where 'near enough is good enough'. Notice your inner dialogue – how do you speak to yourself? Apply this to the current situation.

- Imagine that success requires five failures, so the faster you fail the faster you would succeed. What would you do differently?

SUMMARY

- Engagement is undermined.

- The prevailing perception is that staff are not trusted.

- The direct report's driving intention is to maintain high standards.

- Possible drivers? They may have low trust; a high need for detail; an insistence on overly high standards; a reluctance to release control or are a perfectionist.

Poker face
showing no emotion

**"Your face is a book,
where men may read strange matters."
William Shakespeare**

There's a parallel world of communication if only you tune into it. Communication is way more than the spoken word. Relying too heavily on just the words can mean you miss valuable data and are misconstrued by your peers.

She says

People should choose their words carefully.

She thinks

Words matter.
People should choose their words carefully.
Emotion doesn't belong at work.
Let's keep it rational.
I say what I mean and mean what I say.

He thinks

She's disconnected from her stakeholders.
She appears cold and aloof.
She can't read the room.
Everything is black or white with her.

Her intention

Accurate communication.

360 feedback

- I can never tell what she is thinking. I don't trust her.

- She doesn't take a hint. She is so literal. You have to be really specific with what you want or she just doesn't get it.

- I am so overwhelmed with work and she just doesn't seem to notice or care.

- Mary is very unemotional. She can't connect on a personal level.

- She's a hard worker, but seems a bit aloof.

- Mary is very controlled. While on one level I respect that, I just wish she would show some emotion so we know she is human.

- Mary misses the mood of one of our key stakeholders. There have been a number of situations that could have exploded if I were not there to ease the situation.

- She's like a machine, hearing what we say but not really getting it. She needs an emotional translator!

DISCOVER – what's the problem?

Chris watched the interaction from his office. It was Mary and Simon in another discussion. He could see that Simon was getting more and more frustrated as Mary remained cool. He waited for the inevitable complaint to arrive.

Simon burst into Chris's office. "I just can't work with her! She's so hard to read and she just doesn't get it." He couldn't understand why Mary wouldn't acknowledge what was going on. The team was not on board with the changes and yet when Mary checked in with them they all offered up their verbal support. Mary took them at their word and didn't see what was really going on. It was so obvious to Simon – the body language, the tone of voice, the eye contact, but Mary just didn't pick it up.

DECODE – what's the cause?

MARY

Mary is someone who values straight talk. She is focused on the meaning of the words, believing that is the key to real understanding. Her face is often expressionless and she doesn't see the value in emotive communication. She is sometimes accused of not 'getting it', whatever 'it' is.

Mary is often heard saying things like, "Choose your words carefully" or asking, "What's in the fine print?". She is also known in the department for her mantra: "The workplace is no place for emotions".

Mary's intention is to communicate as accurately as possible and being very deliberate about her vocabulary choice is the best way she knows how to do that. She knows that emotions can cloud judgment, so she ensures that her own mood is constant and discourages others from being emotional at work.

The unintended consequence of being such a literal communicator is that she often misses important nonverbal cues from others. She fails to read the subtext of a situation and misses hints from those who communicate more inferentially through facial expressions, tonality and body language in general. Her reliance on the spoken words rather than the way they are communicated means she is often misjudged as aloof, reserved and even cold. People find her hard to read and hard to connect with as a result.

CHRIS

Chris knows that Mary is misunderstood. He observes a disconnection between her and key stakeholders. He notices that it takes a long time for people to get to know her, and for Mary to develop influence. As a presenter, Mary's mono-tonal voice quickly sends audiences to sleep. Colleagues have complained that she is pedantic in communication, often correcting others on what has been said.

Chris also knows that Mary struggles to read the room and pick up on subtle cues in the communication. It is costing her but Mary can't see it. Mary is unintentionally putting people offside and people don't trust her because they can't tell what she is thinking.

Chris often observes Mary's team members scowling or sighing in exasperation after an interaction with her. She has a tendency to be black and white. Her clients prefer to deal with her team members than go directly to her because they feel she isn't welcoming.

On top of that, she is developing a bad reputation as a result, which is unfair because she is a good person who works hard.

TEAM

Mary's team experience her as cold, unemotional and disconnected from them. They know she is skilled and good at her job but some members believe she never notices when they are stressed or struggling and therefore doesn't care enough offer to help or support. Even when they drop hints about what's going on, she seems oblivious or unwilling to acknowledge the real situation. It feels like she just doesn't care.

When they put proposals to her, they find it challenging to interpret whether they have hit the mark. Some members of the team feel she is negatively judging them.

SOME POSSIBLE CAUSES

Missing nonverbal cues

Communication is more than just words. Understanding the complete intended message is as much about hearing the words as it is about noticing and interpreting the way those words are delivered.

When leaders tune in to the content of the message (words only), they can miss the all-important subtext that is often communicated through nonverbal channels including facial expressions, tonality and body language. Without the subtext to fill in the gaps in communication, leaders are in danger of missing vital cues about what is really going on, as so much of communication occurs through inference from these non-verbal channels. This also affects their ability to build rapport with others, as rapport requires an ability to notice and respond to nonverbal cues, among other things.

Unexpressive communication

Communication requires signposting along the way. Clear communication involves an ability to let others know how the communication is progressing.

Effective leaders signal to those they speak with that they are listening, paying attention and processing the communication. They use nonverbal communication such as facial expressions, nodding and body language. These cues provide the signals required for others to feel heard and understood.

When leaders fail to provide these important communication cues others can misjudge them as being uninterested, uncaring or just not 'getting it'.

DESIGN – what's the action?

SNAPSHOT OF CURRENT THINKING

Communication is central to the success of every organisation. Failures in organisations and relationships can always be traced back to a failure to communicate.[77]

Daniel Goleman, who popularised the concepts of emotional intelligence and social intelligence, states, "When it comes to leadership, or success more broadly in many of our endeavors – what you achieve depends on *everyone else being effective*, so you need to be successful by influencing, persuading, developing, growing, inspiring and motivating other people. That's the social intelligence ability. It requires empathy and it requires skilled interaction."[78]

It is not just what you say and how you say it, but also how well you have understood the social context. Matthew Lieberman at UCLA also made the important discovery that we are wired for connection and so therefore, when not engaged in a task, our social brain is actively engaged scanning our environment and preparing for our next social interaction.[79] An even more important finding from this study was that the analytical brain (pre-frontal cortex) and the social brain, represented through a series of structures in the midline of the brain, do not operate simultaneously. When one is on, the other is off, creating a neural see-saw. So in order to be holistic in our communication we need to be adept in switching in and out of these thinking centres to assess both the verbal and nonverbal cues.

Scientific studies have also discovered that humans make judgments about a person's trustworthiness within the first 500 milliseconds of hearing their voice. The psychologists from the universities of Glasgow, Scotland and Princeton in the US, have shown that a simple "Hello" is sufficient to allow most people to draw conclusions about personality type, even without seeing the person to whom they are speaking.[80] The findings of the study suggests that the tone of voice that you use when you say "Hello" directly informs the first impression of you made by the person to whom you are speaking. Dr Phil McAleer, from the Voice Neurocognition Laboratory, University of Glasgow, who led the study, states: "It is amazing that from such short bursts of speech you can get such a definite impression of a person. And more so that, irrespective of whether it is accurate, your impression is the same as what the other listeners get. It is perhaps also consistent that we are most attuned to recognising signs of trustworthiness and dominance, two traits that would have been central to our survival as we evolved."

Carol Kinsey Goman, author of *The Silent Language of Leaders: How Body Language Can Help — or Hurt — How You Lead* states there are two sets of signals a person gives off.[81] The first signal is one of status and authority; the next gives off warmth and empathy. Kinsey Goman offers a range of tips for successful collaboration, and here are three that are relevant for Poker Face:

1. **Activate your smile power.** A smile can tell others how approachable, cooperative and trustworthy you are.

2. **Use your head.** Kinsey Goman found people speak more if "the listener nods in clusters of three at regular intervals". Tilting your head also shows you are involved and interested.

3. **Look at people when they speak.** People will feel like they have your attention as long as you're making eye contact. Avoid being distracted by phones or other people.

As leaders move from being transactional to transformational, the ability to influence others has become increasingly more important.

There is a body of research however that supports the notion that more expressive communication is more effective when we are seeking to be persuasive. In the *Harvard Business Review* article, 'Learning Charisma', the researchers identify three nonverbal cues that are key to charisma: expressions of voice, body and face. While they don't come naturally to all, they are highly effective for showing passion and winning over listeners.

1. **Animated voice.** People who are passionate vary the volume and emotions they communicate through their speech. They also use pauses for conveying control.

2. **Facial expressions.** Helping to reinforce your message, facial expressions help listeners to see as well as hear your message. Eye contact is key.

3. **Gestures.** Like listening signposts, hand gestures can be used to reinforce emotion or to draw attention at different points of the communication.

We think Kinsey Goman summarises the concept of effective communication well when she states, "There's no good or bad body language signal." Rather, she suggests that it depends on what your message is as to whether your body language supports or sabotages the message.

COACHING TIPS TO INCREASE EXPRESSION IN COMMUNICATION

Learning to read nonverbal cues

- Interview someone who is good at building rapport easily with others. Ask them what nonverbal cues they watch for and how they respond when they see them. Choose one nonverbal signal for a week to observe and implement into your communication.

- When your team member's body language does not align with their words consider what questions you could ask to build your understanding of their true perspective?

- It is widely accepted that nonverbal communication accounts for a significant portion of the meaning of the message. What vital information might you have missed through overlooking nonverbal cues?

- Watch TV for 10 minutes with the sound down and notice what understanding you gain without hearing the words. What emotions are being expressed?

- Develop your ability to recognise facial expressions and their meanings through specialised training in micro-expressions.

- Develop your understanding and recognition of the nonverbal cues of others by reading materials on body language. Focus on observing these cues in your workplace.

- How does your professional training influence you to focus more on the content and less on the nonverbal cues of others? How could you expand your search for 'data' beyond the words to the nonverbal signals of others?

Being more expressive

- How would a more expressive approach in the delivery of your message enhance your outcomes?

- What is the culture of your workplace? How accepted is the expression of emotions and feelings generally? What does this mean for building relationships with others?

- What level of animation was appropriate in your home growing up? How is this impacting your current communication in the workplace?

- What could you do differently to be more emotionally 'visible' to others? What will you attempt this week?

- Have someone video you as you communicate with others. Replaying the video, notice what expressions are showing on your face and through your body movements and hand gestures.

What else could you incorporate in order to convey your message without using words?

- When practising being more expressive, use bigger expressions and gestures than you feel comfortable with and notice the positive response you get. Even though you may be uncomfortable, others may be pleasantly surprised at how engaged you appear to them. The more you do this, the easier it gets.

- Identify a collegue or friend who is good at nonverbal communciation. Ask them to observe you and provide specific real-time feedback about your nonverbal signalling.

SUMMARY

- Emotions are hard to read.
- The prevailing perception is that they are cold and hard to connect with.
- The direct report's driving intention is to focus on what is said, not how it's said.
- Possible drivers? They may miss nonverbal cues or use limited facial expressions.

People burner
poor people skills

"**Today we are faced with the pre-eminent fact that, if civilization is to survive, we must cultivate the science of human relationships.**"
Franklin D. Roosevelt

A focus on the outcome over relationship limits potential. Outcomes at the expense of connection equal short-lived success. Real connection with people unlocks discretionary effort and drives full engagement.

She says

I'm not here to make friends.

She thinks

We're here to get the job done.
Your emotions are your business.
People should be judged on their competence to deliver.
We should all work hard to get this done.

He thinks

She's lacking in soft skills.
People are put off side by her behaviour.
I'm worried about the potential for perception of bullying.
People are trying to work around her.
There's a loss of good people from her team.

Her intention
Get results.

360 feedback

- She is prepared to sacrifice relationships to get the job done.

- She doesn't understand what's really going on.

- I don't like the way she speaks to me.

- She is detached and aloof – it's no fun being in this team.

- I am embarrassed by her behaviour and inappropriate comments in client meetings.

- I avoid Mary wherever I can and find some other way of getting the information I need.

- The only feedback we ever get is negative.

DISCOVER – what's the problem?

Mary banged her fist on the conference table to emphasise her point – everyone needed to do what was required to get the project over the line. The deadlines were tight, the client was expecting success and the project revenue was critical to achieving budget.

Chris glanced around the table at the body language of some of the project team; faces darkening and some physically withdrawing. He knew that Mary's intentions were good. Mary's strong focus on revenue and delivery was part of the last 18 months' success. She had high standards for herself and drove her team hard too.

Chris sighed when he remembered the bullying claim outstanding in his inbox. Mary often put people off side but this time she had gone too far. Very few people in her team liked her. Team morale was low and no one put in discretionary effort any more. Key members of her team sought answers from other executives rather than speaking to Mary. Mary seems oblivious to this. Unless she learns to relate to her team quickly, all the results she has achieved so far will be rapidly undone.

DECODE – what's the cause?

MARY

Mary values competency and is highly goal orientated. She focuses on getting results. She knows that the workplace is not the appropriate place to display emotions; we are all well paid to get the job done. She understands that sometimes people take her the 'wrong way' and believes that her track record of successful delivery is what she should be judged by.

Mary can often be heard bemoaning the fact that her team don't work as hard as she does, despite her role modelling, self-discipline and focus.

She can be heard to say, "I am not here to make friends; we are here to get a job done".

Mary's intention is to get results. She pushes herself hard and pushes her team in the same way. The unintended consequences of her approach include high turnover, low morale and no discretionary effort in her team, as well as burnt bridges and reduced ability to influence across the organisation.

CHRIS

Chris can always rely on Mary to hit her targets, and yet he wishes he could give her a simple injection of 'soft skills'. She has the potential to be the next CEO if only she can learn to relate to people. There have been times when he has reflected back to her what she has said, and her "What's wrong with that?" is accompanied by a puzzled look. It's often as if she is blind to the nonverbal feedback from the team.

Other times her strong focus means she thinks it's okay to burn people along the way. Then when they leave her team she's quick to judge them as unable to keep up the pace. At least two significant mistakes could have been avoided recently if she was willing to listen to her team. A few clients have commented on her abrupt nature.

TEAM

Mary's team experience her as uncaring and unsupportive. While a few people begrudgingly admire her results focus, most see her lack of interest in people and relationships as limiting project results in the long term. Almost all team members have a story to tell of how Mary has belittled them in public when a project deliverable didn't meet her standard, or when they expressed reluctance to work yet another late night to get a job complete.

Few people have the confidence to tell Mary when they disagree with a decision. Disagreement is seen as a career-limiting move unless Mary can immediately see how this will save time and achieve the result faster. Consequently, they withhold ideas, poor decisions are implemented and people feel disempowered. Her lack of ability or willingness to provide feedback means that people see joining her team as a career-limiting move.

SOME POSSIBLE CAUSES

Lacking warmth and empathy

Warmth and empathy are fundamental to strong people skills. A leader who is not emotionally expressive, and misses the nonverbal cues about how the communication is progressing, often fails to connect with people around them. They may be perceived as cold, slightly aloof or stand-offish, or unable to take a hint.

This leader focuses their communication towards the content (the exact words that are said) or the information they get and what they think about that content. They may appear to others as someone who is pedantic about the specifics of the content. They can become known for taking things too literally and not building relationships with people around them.

Focus on achievement at the expense of relationships

Strong leadership requires a focus on people and results. A leader who is overly focused on achievement or goals can appear to others as someone who cares more about the task than the people. A sole focus on achievement can result in poor work-life balance, damage to relationships with stakeholders and colleagues, loss of productivity, etc.

Their strong outcome focus can lead them to believe that people are obstacles to be overcome in achieving their outcome. Their high standards may result in them driving themselves too hard, being reluctant to delegate and suffering burnout.

Poor social cognition

The ability to read the emotions of others and the social environment is an adaptive advantage as a leader. Social intelligence, a subset of emotional intelligence or EQ, enables a leader to read a social environment and then respond. Socially intelligent leaders are firstly able to sense what others are feeling and their intentions. Secondly, they have the social skills to act on that information.

Poor self control

We all have feral tendencies. The mark of leadership, like statesmanship, is to choose when to display your inner feral and when to keep it under control!

This leader may 'explode' without self-censorship, damaging relationships and leaving those in his wake to deal with the explosion. Their inability to control their emotional state will impact their own productivity as well as the productivity of those around them.

Win-at-all-costs mentality

The means justifies the end. A leader who is willing to accept any 'how' to achieve the 'what', may feel justified in overlooking the importance of relationships. A focus on self with the absence of a focus on others is also likely to reduce performance.

Socially awkward

The intention is positive yet the skill is lacking. Some people are socially awkward – despite the best of intentions, this leader makes social overtures that are open to misinterpretation.

This leader may have a strong commitment to people and a strong belief in the value of relationships, and yet often make social faux pas' that seem to contradict social norms.

DESIGN – what's the action?

SNAPSHOT OF CURRENT THINKING

Success in relationships means success in business.

Leaders need to focus on people and tasks. According to neuroscientist, Matthew Lieberman[82], social skills are a multiplier. A leader with strong people skills can leverage the technical abilities of team members far more effectively. As Lieberman suggests, "often what initially appear to be task-related difficulties turn out to be interpersonal problems in disguise". Socially skilled leaders are better at diagnosing and treating these common workplace dilemmas.

Daniel Goleman,[83] considered a pioneer in the field of emotional intelligence, highlights in a *Harvard Business Review* podcast that success in leadership depends on your team being effective. You become successful by "influencing, persuading, developing, growing, inspiring, motivating other people". This is known as social intelligence.

Social intelligence means being smart **about** relationships. It means being empathetic. It's sensing what the other person is feeling, understanding their point of view. It's ease and facility in having smooth, effective interactions. So it's both knowing what the person is feeling and acting effectively based on that. Daniel Goleman's research has confirmed "that there is a large performance gap between socially intelligent and socially unintelligent leaders".[84] For example, in working with a national bank, Goleman found "that levels of an executive's social intelligence competencies predicted yearly performance appraisals more powerfully than did the emotional intelligence competencies of self-awareness and self-management".[85]

Poor people skills can create stressful environments hampering performance

The recent discovery of mirror neurons has shown that we are wired to detect and mirror the emotions of others. Put simply, emotions are contagious, and toxic and stressful environments can infect the mood and cognitive performance of everyone. Just like bad news travels fast, bad moods also travel fast. The brain perceives a threat five times faster than a reward[86] and this generates a fight or flight response. Biochemical changes then limit a person's ability to regulate emotions and think rationally. The result is confusion, less effective decision-making, negative group dynamics and reduced productivity and effectiveness. Consequently, leaders want to have good people skills that foster positive working environments.

Focusing on others and how we are helping them motivates us to work harder

Dr. Adam Grant is a professor at the University of Pennsylvania and undertook a study that showed that helping others, motivates us to work harder. In his book, *Give and Take*, he describes his study that involved staff at a university whose job was to make calls to university alumni to raise money for undergraduate scholarships.

Grant staged an intervention where some of these callers received a surprise visit from a past scholarship recipient, who had directly benefitted from the work that they do. The visits were only of five minutes' duration. At the end of that time the manager said, "Remember this when you are on the phone; this is someone you are supporting."

It would be expected that this intervention might improve performance for the rest of the day. However, by tracking their performance data over the weeks that followed, Grant found that improved performance was sustained a month later and had resulted in a 171 per cent increase in donations. An outstanding outcome given that all he did was remind people how their work was helping others.

Grant then ran a complementary study. In this study, he gave one group of callers a letter that explained how their work helped them *personally* and the second group got a letter describing how their work benefitted scholarship recipients. Those with the self-focus *did not change their performance*. Those focused on others once again showed dramatic gains – the number of donations increased 153 per cent and the donation value increased by 143 per cent.

Grant's work, which has been replicated with consistent results, reinforces the very simple construct that when we can see how what we do helps other people, we are more engaged, work harder, care more about the organisation we are working for and produce better outcomes.

COACHING TIPS TO INCREASE YOUR PEOPLE FOCUS

Build warmth and empathy

- What three nonverbal signals could you focus on today?
- How would a more expressive approach in the delivery of your message connect you to people and enhance your outcomes?
- Watch a TV show with the sound turned down and 'read' the emotions and conversational subtext. Build this skill through television and then apply it in the workplace.
- Notice when your team members' body language does not align with their words. What questions could you ask to build your understanding of their true perspective and add that into your focus on the task?
- Take some time to learn more about the people with whom you work – what is important to them at work and outside of work? How can you demonstrate your interest in them as an individual?
- How could you show appreciation of, and interest in, your colleagues today?
- What could be gained by expressing your own vulnerability as a human and as a leader?
- Carl W. Buechner said, "They may forget what you said, but they will never forget how you made them feel." For one day, accept that this is true and notice how this impacts your work relationships.

Focus on relationships as well as achievement

- What are you afraid will happen if you reduce your focus on achieving the results?

- What is the cost to you of downplaying the importance of relationships and people connections?

- How could you build greater harmony within your work group?

- Think of someone you know who you could describe as being focused on 'win at all costs'. What collateral damage have you seen from their style?

- What would be the impact on your current role or project if you were 10 per cent more focused on fostering collaboration and harmony within the team?

- Observe the strengths of the people in your team. How do these individual strengths benefit the team as a whole? How well are you appreciating and utilising those strengths now?

- What would you do right now if the most important thing was having positive and mutually supportive relationships with your colleagues?

- For three weeks, focus more on how you can help others and less on how they can help you. Observe any differences in your relationships and in the outcomes you are achieving.

Develop social cognition

- Consciously take notice of the people around you. Notice the dynamics between them and the emotions they appear to be displaying.

- Develop an attentiveness towards other people, as if the value of the organisational 'social life' was just as important as the results. Notice how this builds the relationships that will offer you more data about the situation.

- Monitor your own reactions over one week; pause to reflect before offering a measured response in social situations. Notice what you learn from that.

- Identify a colleague who has strong people skills, and debrief with them on the unspoken dynamics after meetings.
- Solicit feedback about interpersonal exchanges, including specific comments and suggestions of what you might have missed and alternative ways for response in future.

Increase self-control

- Understand what you are responding to and reframe issues to reduce the emotional charge.
- Press the 'pause button'. Take 30 seconds to reconsider the situation before responding.
- If you find yourself in an emotionally charged situation, walk away rather than exploding with an unhelpful emotional response. Re-engage when you are calm.
- Take three deep breaths before responding.
- Imagine there was a response to this situation that would build the relationship. What is it?

Develop a win-win mentality

- What's the worst that could happen if you didn't win right now?
- Whose voice do you hear in your head when you consider success? What insight does that give you? How could you let this voice go and develop your own position?
- How could the need to win be preventing you from winning?
- Tom Krause said, "Courage is the discovery that you may not win, and trying when you know you can lose." What would it take for you to believe that? What will become possible when you do?

Expand social skills

- Observe others who have excellent social skills. What can you learn from them?

- Take a peer into your confidence and ask for their support. Request real-time feedback on how they observe you in social situations, and what you might do differently in response.

- Keep practising. No one learns a new skill without practice. (Remember when you first learned to ride a bike?) You may fall off a few times and that's part of the learning curve.

SUMMARY

- Performance outweighs people.
- The prevailing perception is of not caring and being unsupportive.
- The direct report's driving intention is to get results.
- Possible drivers? They may be lacking in warmth and empathy; have a focus on performance over people; have poor social cognition or poor self-control; have a win-at-all-costs mentality; are possibly socially awkward.

Tactician
poor strategic thinker

"Thinking is the greatest torture in the world for most people."
Voltaire

The doing doesn't determine the direction. Focusing on the tactical here and now, at the expense of the strategic, leaves you behind the eight ball. An ability to conceptualise alternative futures and look beyond the here and now creates the opportunity to stay competitive.

She says

We're on track for now.

She thinks

Current client needs are paramount.
Let's just get through today.
This is the right way.
All bases are covered.

He thinks

She has no vision for the future.
She is uncomfortable with uncertainty.
She lacks imagination and foresight.

Her intention

Delivering outcomes now.

360 feedback

- We don't know what to say "no" or "yes" to without a strategy.

- Doing more of the same is not a strategy!

- Mary has no idea of trends in the industry or what's coming up – I expect more from a senior manager.

- It's a highly reactive environment and we are falling behind our competitors

- Mary thinks good customer service is a strategy – that's just the price of entry now.

- Mary was shocked by the recent merger between two of our competitors, but it was so bleedingly obvious to most of us! And Mary hasn't even considered our place in the market as a result.

- Her eyes glaze over when we talk about anything further away than next week.

- She is more in the detail than any senior manager I have worked with before.

- I was excited when I heard Mary was coming to lead our section. Now I would love to change departments.

DISCOVER – what's the problem?

Chris throws the papers down on his desk in frustration. He has just finished reading the end-of-quarter reports, and while the organisation overall is travelling well, the business unit run by Mary is taking an unprecedented battering. Clearly Mary's unit is in desperate need of a solid strategy to get them out of this slump.

Mary was viewed by everyone as a rising star of the business, who delivers excellent results without exception. On the back of her success, Mary had been promoted to lead her unit 12 months ago. Chris was conscious of the fact that much of Mary's success had been achieved through operational roles, so in their first meeting after her appointment he had emphasised the need for her to get off the tools and focus on setting a solid strategy for her team to execute.

Given her experience Chris had not expected any difficulties, but more recently he had observed that whenever strategy was raised in their executive meetings, Mary was very quiet and didn't contribute much at all. He was sure that she knew what to do and was at a loss to understand why she had failed to apply her knowledge and put a good strategic plan in place.

DECODE – what's the cause?

MARY

Mary values delivery of the outcomes her clients need now. This regularly involves in-the-moment troubleshooting to make sure the job gets done and clients are kept happy. By being amongst the action, Mary is better positioned to make sure all bases are covered. She regularly checks in with her team to see whether 'the project is on track'.

Mary's intention is to make sure client satisfaction is maintained by delivering the best job possible. She doesn't understand what Chris means when he keeps asking for her strategy. The way she operates has always been highly effective and kept clients happy. Why would she consider doing it differently?

The unintended consequences of her preference for focusing on the day-to-day operations is that she is failing to grow business for her unit and leverage emerging opportunities. She realises that she should be thinking about the future, but the pressure of dropping the existing balls means she doesn't feel she can afford to take time out for strategic thinking.

CHRIS

Chris appreciates Mary's commitment to client focus, and yet he judges her to be lacking in vision. Nailing the strategy is critical if Mary's unit is to achieve the agreed growth targets, and yet she is spinning wheels maintaining the status quo and is failing to drive the business forward.

Even her team can see another future, and they are frustrated as Mary refuses to consider their ideas or set aside time for planning.

Chris is seriously questioning Mary's fit for this role – she just doesn't seem to have the strategic capability needed for this part of the business.

TEAM

Mary's team are frustrated at her lack of strategic leadership in a changing marketplace. Some believe she can't think conceptually. Others see that she is doing her best and has a lot to offer, but just can't think beyond the day-to-day operations.

One of the biggest concerns is her high attention to detail, and her apparent inability to consider the future. Without a clear strategy, the team is struggling to prioritise opportunities, and Mary's reluctance to move outside the status quo means that opportunities have been lost.

Mary's peers regard her as having an exceptional customer service focus for today's market, and yet question her ability to even imagine that the future may not be the same as the present.

SOME POSSIBLE CAUSES

Inability to think conceptually

Conceptual thinking is a prerequisite for strategic thinking. Conceptual thinking motivates a leader to understand and develop ideas and theories, and/or understand the underlying theoretical concepts.

A leader who does not spend time analysing or theorising concepts is at risk of jumping too soon without being informed. This leader may appear to others as someone who 'acts first and thinks later', and may appear impatient to commence activity and/or prone to disorganisation. Alternatively, they may be so focused on structured planning that they appear to value the plan more than the conceptual thinking behind it.

A leader who focuses on planning, organising the resources, detailing the dependencies and timing etc, or who prioritises taking immediate action before understanding the theoretical context, is in danger of moving in the wrong direction.

Inability to accept or generate alternatives

Strategic thinking requires the ability to generate alternatives beyond current practice. A leader who believes there is a correct or best way of doing something may be demotivated to develop or accept new possibilities, and be limited in seeing what is beyond today.

This leader may appear to others as someone who is dogmatic, shows little flexibility, or is rigid in their thinking. Their commitment to process may prevent them from developing strategic alternatives or anticipating the opportunities and challenges ahead.

Tactical rather than strategic focus

Putting aside today's tactical work is vital for strategic thinking. A leader who focuses exclusively on their current workload and maintains an operational focus will struggle to move into a strategic space.

When achieving quick wins in the here and now is much more motivating than imagining a possible future, strategic thinking is hard to achieve. This leader may be recognised for their preference for getting stuff done in the moment, rather than thinking into the future. Others may see them as being stuck in the operational detail and unable to see the bigger picture.

Struggles to see market patterns

A strategic leader can interpret market trends and patterns. Activity in the current marketplace provides strategic indicators for the future, only when they can be interpreted. Sense-making is a critical tool for strategy. A leader who is unable to connect and interpret current market murmuring with how their business operates now and into the future may be caught out by 'unanticipated' market shifts.

Others may see this leader as being focused on the present at the expense of the future. Their inability to interpret what is going on around them and see the potential impacts on the way their business currently operates could be viewed as lacking insight and sense-making ability.

Inability to think broadly

Strategy is not born in the detail. Strategic thinking requires a big-picture approach, and a focus on detail will limit the development of strategy.

A leader who prefers a focus on detail could appear to others as someone who spends too much time working at the micro level, and who appears to focus energy on things that are not strategically important.

Discomfort with ambiguity

Strategy by its very nature is ambiguous and uncertain. Fear of the unknown and discomfort with ambiguity can limit strategic thinking.

A leader who is uncomfortable with ambiguity may avoid thinking strategically, preferring to focus on things more concrete and known. This leader could appear to others as only trading in certainties and reluctant to play the strategic planning game.

DECODE – what's the action?

SNAPSHOT OF CURRENT THINKING

Research completed at the Wharton School and Decision Strategies International involving more than 20,000 executives identified six skills that, when mastered and implemented together, facilitate strategic thinking and navigation of the unknown. Strategic leaders have the ability to:

- Anticipate

- Challenge

- Interpret

- Decide

- Align

- Learn

Described in detail in the *Harvard Business Review* article, Strategic Leadership: The Essential Skills[87] the article defines an adaptive strategic leader as "someone who is both resolute and flexible, persistent in the face of setbacks but also able to react strategically to environmental shifts" and "has learned to apply all six [skills] at once".

To better **anticipate**, it is suggested that leaders talk to stakeholders to understand their challenges, do research, scenario-planning, focus groups, assess the competition, seek to better understand lost business and network across industries.

To better **challenge**, look at the cause not the symptoms and ask the 'five whys'[88]. Identify and list longstanding assumptions and test these across a diverse group for truth. Encourage debate, create rotating positions, include naysayers in the decision process and capture input from those not directly impacted by the decision.

To better **interpret** ambiguous data, look for at least three possible explanations for the observations and invite diverse perspective. Look at the detail and the big picture and question what might be missing. Then pursue thinking and information that counters your view. Add quantitative analysis and step away occasionally to maintain an open mind.

To better **decide**, consider more options and break down big decisions into smaller parts to better understand the consequences. Adjust your decision criteria for both the long and short term and keep others updated on your progress. Identify who needs to be directly involved and who has influence over your decision. Run pilots where possible before making big commitments.

To better **align**, communicate early and regularly. Identify key stakeholders and understand their perspectives and agendas. Structure and facilitate key discussions then actively engage resisters and address their concerns. Monitor stakeholder perspectives closely and often, and reward and recognise colleagues who support team alignment.

To better **learn**, run post-implementation reviews to incorporate key insights and lessons learned. Reward team members who try something commendable but whose outcomes fail. Do learning audits. Consider root causes where decisions have fallen short, or where initiatives are not bearing fruit. Foster a culture of learning where constructive questioning and mistakes are seen as valuable learning opportunities.

COACHING TIPS TO INCREASE STRATEGIC THINKING

Think conceptually

- If you were to prioritise developing a conceptual understanding of your current project, what would you do differently right now?

- Why is it important that this task is completed and how does it contribute to your organisation's objectives?

- Metaphors are one type of right brain conceptual thinking. If you were to describe your activities in a metaphor, what would that metaphor be?

- If developing a conceptual understanding was more important than developing resource plans, what would you do first?

- Before starting any task, get clear on the purpose. Write yourself a statement about why you are doing it.

- Before taking action, have a conversation with three key stakeholders about the rationale behind the project request. Use what you learn to develop a concept statement to guide your team.

Generate alternatives

- If there were other ways to do this, what would they be?

- What are five different approaches that could be taken here?

- List the long-standing truths of your area/organisation, and rigorously challenge each one.

- How could you 'break' this process and rebuild it? What are five ways you could do that?

- What possibilities would open up if you considered how to make this smaller/bigger, faster/slower, more detailed/bigger picture, free/twice the price, privately available/publically available?

- When you think you know the best way, identify just one more possibility.

- What if this wasn't the best way? How else could you approach it?

- Every day this week identify one small familiar process you could complete in an alternative way in order to explore other possibilities.

Reduce tactical focus

- If today's operational work was fully taken care of, how would that free up your thinking? Imagine that this was true and see where it takes you.

- What are the future implications of your actions today?

- Where has focusing on the present operational activity limited your ability to foresee future issues? What could you learn from that?

- How could living entirely in the present prevent you from anticipating what might happen in the future?

- How could you improve your effectiveness through a greater focus on the future? What opportunities await you?

- Read the blogs of some futurists. Allow yourself to play in their world for a while. Notice how that influences your thinking.

- Talk to key stakeholders to understand their challenges and what they are likely to want and need in the future.

Navigate market trends

- If there was a link between what is happening today in the market and your organisation's potential downfall next year, what would that be? What would you do today to mitigate against that?

- Imagine there was an opportunity in this week's news for your company. What is it?

- What patterns can you see in market behaviour? What implications do they have for your key product?

- Question what data might be missing and pursue points of view that are counter to your view. What can you learn from that?

- Learn about the growth cycle of another industry, and imagine what would happen if that applied to your sector.

- Read market analysis in the business section of the newspaper to understand relevant market trends.

- Identify someone in your professional network who appears well informed about market trends. Ask them what media sources they consult to inform their thinking, and consult these sources.

Reduce detail focus

- Speak to a colleague or manager who considers the future in broad terms. Learn how they do it.

- Assume you have all the detail you need already. What decision would you make right now?

- If you feel lost in the detail, zoom out and look for the major patterns or principles. Ask yourself what is the purpose of this activity.

- What are the essential concepts you need to focus on, to move out of the detail into the realm of the strategic?

- As a person becomes more senior in an organisation, with broader responsibilities and competing demands on their time, they typically become less detailed and more big picture. How can you ensure you let go of the detail in order to think strategically?

- Free yourself to embrace a broader perspective by surrounding yourself with people who can competently manage the detail for you so you can consider the future.

- Ask yourself: "What's the bottom line here?" after each statement you want to make. Keep asking this in your head until you get to the main assumptions that will support your thinking.

Get comfortable with ambiguity

- Get clear on some key assumptions to anchor your thinking and underpin your strategy.

- How does a need for certainty affect your ability to think strategically? What would you do if you thrived in uncertainty?

- What is available to you from letting go of the need for certainty?

- What is the downside of certainty when it comes to conceptualising the future?

- Imagine 'black' and 'white' were your enemy, and you loved 'grey'. What would you do next?

- Where in the past did you proceed despite the ambiguity? How could you apply that experience to your current situation?

- When analysing ambiguous data, look for at least three possible explanations for your observations and invite others with diverse perspectives to comment.

SUMMARY

- Inability to capitalise on future possibilities.

- The prevailing perception is a lack of direction.

- The direct report's driving intention is to deliver outcomes now.

- Possible drivers? They may have an inability to think conceptually or to accept or generate alternatives; they are tactical rather than strategic; they struggle to see market patterns; they have an inability to think broadly or have a discomfort with ambiguity.

Wild Card questions, coaching tips and activities

Just like the wild card in the card game Uno, these Wild Card coaching tips can apply to almost any situation. The Wild Card coaching tips have activities and reflective questions that you can apply to any derailer. You may find that one of these is particularly relevant for your direct report's current challenge.

You might also find that building a vocabulary of these Wild Card questions is useful in everyday leadership situations. There is no need to wait for a performance management conversation.

Get clear on desired outcome

- What does success look like? How will you recognise this once you've achieved it?
- What outcome do you want from this (conversation, activity, initiative)?
- What is your goal?
- What's important for you to experience as a result of this?
- Who will this allow you to be at the end?
- Who else will benefit from you shifting?

Explore reality

- What's important to you/your team/your stakeholders at the moment?
- What's working well for you at the moment?
- What isn't working well at the moment?
- What have you done so far to improve things?
- What's the excuse that you have used for not achieving X?

- What is the biggest obstacle that you are facing?

- What are you afraid of?

- What new reality are you avoiding?

- What are you passionate about?

- What would be the most helpful thing that you could do now?

- Where are you already doing this new behaviour right now? How could you apply this to your current situation?

Understand impact

- How might others perceive your behaviour?

- What's the impact of this behaviour on your results?

- How might the behaviour be holding you back?

- What's the potential impact on your professional reputation and career of others' perception of your behaviour?

- How are others experiencing you right now?

- What's the potential impact on stakeholder relationships and the organisational brand?

- What is this focus costing you?

- If you knew your 360-degree feedback results were going to be on the front page news tomorrow, what would you do differently now?

- Imagine that you can only see yourself through your stakeholders' eyes on your worst day – how would they describe you? What can you learn from this?

Know what drives you

- What does the *present state** get you?

- What have you used the *present state* to avoid?

- What have you used the *present state* for?

- What would you have to face if you didn't have the *present state*?

- What have you used the *present state* to justify?

- What have you used the *present state* to be/do/have?

- What have you used the *present state* to not be/do/have?'

*(Present state refers to the current challenge you're aiming to shift.)

Change perspective

- Consider the issue from different perspectives: time, space, role, outcome, professional background, etc. For example:

- Imagine it was six months from now. Look back and describe …

- Imagine seeing this situation from a regional/city/local/global perspective. What could you do…?

- Imagine you were the CEO/your best customer/Richard Branson/ Madonna. What could you do…?

- What would have to be true for you to change the way you think about this?

- If you had 50 per cent more confidence, what would you be doing that would be different?

- If you weren't holding anything back, what would you be doing?

- If you were guaranteed to succeed, what would you do?

Role model interview/modelling

- Interview someone who demonstrates the qualities you wish to improve. What do they believe? How do they think? What do they focus on? What do they ignore? What do they do/not do? What's important to them? What do they often say? What's been their biggest lesson around this topic? What do they wish someone had told them earlier about this topic?

- Watch someone who learns well from others. Talk to them about how they do that and adopt at least one of their behaviours.

- Visit, watch and explore the work and habits of other people. What do they do that you can take on, learn from and think differently about?
- If you saw someone else in your situation, what would you suggest they do?
- Imagine you are (insert someone you admire for the thing you want to be able to do). What would they do in this situation?

Explore outcomes and consequences

- What will happen if you do ... (behaviour – e.g. micro manage)?
- What won't happen if you do ... (behaviour – e.g. micro manage)?
- What will happen if you don't ... (behaviour – e.g. micro manage)?
- What won't happen if you don't ... (behaviour – e.g. micro manage)?

Next action questions

- What's the best use of your time at the moment?
- If you could only do one thing this week, what would it be?
- What are you going to do in the next 24 hours?
- How will you ensure you do what you say you were going to do?
- What would you do right now if you knew you couldn't fail?
- What roadblocks do you expect or need to plan for? What are some ways to overcome them?
- What would you do if you weren't answerable to anyone?

Marshall Goldsmith's Feedforward

This activity is based on Marshall Goldsmith's feedforward. You can learn more about Marshall Goldsmith at http://www.marshallgoldsmithlibrary.com.

Explain to your direct report that you are going to support them in their leadership development by asking them to seek out information in the form of feedforward.

1. Ask your direct report to pick one behaviour that they would like to change. Change in this behaviour should make a significant, positive difference. For example: I want to be more 'hands off' as a leader.

   2. Encourage them to seek out feedforward from people who they believe can provide them with valuable insight by asking the following: Can you please provide me with two suggestions for the future that might help me achieve a positive change in [x] (their selected behaviour)? Those who are sought out should be advised not to provide feedback on the past but simply to focus on suggestions to facilitate the desired future behaviours.

   3. Your direct report is not to critique the suggestions but must simply respond by saying, "Thank you."

   4. Once these suggestions are gathered together, they can be used as discussion points for future development conversations.

SUMMARY

- The Wild Card coaching tips have activities and reflective questions that you can apply to any derailer.

- Building a vocabulary of these Wild Card questions is useful in everyday leadership situations.

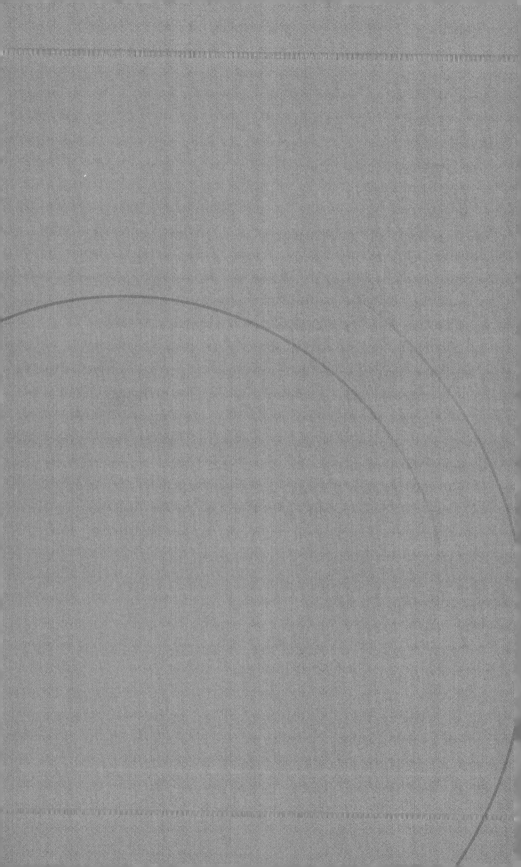

Part 4

More On The Imperative To Change Leadership Development Right Now

Developing direct reports requires new thinking

In part one we talked about why the leadership of leaders needs to change. This is a critical subject and there is more to be said. It is not just about developing the skills to lead leadership. It's about the cultural imperative to change the way we view the dynamics of development in general. It's more than a classroom solution. It's about what leaders can do on a daily basis to develop their leaders on the job, and why they must.

Developing leaders is not a simple exercise. The need for leaders to constantly adapt requires an approach to leadership development that is equally flexible.

While books, study programs and traditional leadership development programs are accessible to most leaders, the usual solutions offered are not tailored to specific development needs, and often don't deliver the intended results.

The development culture within organisations has to progress beyond generic, classroom-based programs to development that primarily occurs on the job.

Adaptive change is key

Creating new leadership behaviours typically requires new ways of thinking as well as new ways of behaving. A change that requires new ways of thinking, and being, is known as an adaptive change. Whereas a change that only requires new skill is known as a technical change.

Too often, leadership development programs respond to an adaptive challenge, i.e. behaviour change, with a technical solution, i.e. getting more knowledge. We know that knowing more doesn't always translate into doing differently because we are not addressing the underlying causes of the original behaviour.

Two types of change – adaptive and technical

An adaptive change is where the solution is unknown. Adaptive change requires exploring new ways of thinking and being that lead to new behavioural choices. It takes time to develop through an evolving cycle of insight, application, reflection and revision.

A technical change is a change where the solution is known and therefore easier to make. Gaining new knowledge or skill is all that is required.[89]

For example, learning skills required for effective time management is often addressed as a technical change. It's assumed that when skills are known they will be applied. However, if you are not actioning the steps despite knowing them, you are facing an adaptive change.

Heiftez, and Linsky[90], in *Leadership on the Line,* say "Indeed, the single most common source of leadership failure we've been able to identify – in politics, community life, business, or the non-profit sector – is that people, especially those in positions of authority, treat adaptive change like technical problems."

Recognition of leadership development requiring adaptive change and not just technical change is critical for successful leadership development to occur.

Traditional corporate training and development doesn't deliver

Along with recognising that adaptive change is required for leadership development to occur, is the need to recognise that adaptive change can't be fostered in a classroom alone. Adaptive change requires focused attention over time and must therefore be encouraged, supported and reinforced by the leader back on the job.

Apart from traditional classroom-based training not allowing sufficient time or exposure for new ideas and ways of thinking to take root, traditional development approaches suffer from other issues also, as outlined below.

This is not to say that stand-alone training is ineffective or unimportant. We are saying that corporate over-reliance on training programs can be a trap.

Five reasons training programs fail

Organisations are investing billions of dollars in learning and development without careful consideration of the business impacts. Often, training and development results are not clear while learning and development costs are increasing. There needs to be a better alignment with business needs and demonstrable return on investment.

Sending your leaders on a training course as a single development strategy won't address performance issues, nor create adaptive leadership changes. Recent studies on the effectiveness of leadership development programs have illustrated the key reasons why traditional leadership development programs fail.

*Let it be known! As performance consultants who write, coach AND train, we are not against training. We are against stand-alone training events **for developing an adaptive leadership change.***

1. **Content is loose**[89]

   Training content is often too generic, with solutions catering for the masses but not necessarily for an individual's actual needs. It is also more focused on the skill set than the mindset, therefore not targeting adaptive changes. There can also be a focus on the theoretical understanding or 'knowing about' the right behaviours rather than focusing on producing the 'habit of doing' the right behaviours. And finally, most content is not strategically linked to business outcomes and therefore hard to embed in real work. Skills are taught without reference to the specific current needs of the business.

2. **Formal learning has limited impact**

Only 15 per cent of formal learning is applied back on the job and studies show that this has not changed since 1975.[92] This is simply because a one-off training event provides no time for adaptive changes to take hold. Consequently, when surveyed, 50 per cent of HR executives said their "leadership development programs were not very effective or didn't provide much lasting benefit."[93]

3. **Application environment is unsupportive**[94]

The work environment a leader goes back to after a training event needs to support the reinforcement and integration of new behaviours. Otherwise the lessons learnt are not reinforced or developed properly back on the job[95]. The culture of the organisation, the team and, most of all, the line manager, have a huge part to play in creating a supportive or unsupportive environment for the application of learning post training.

Follow up the follow-up

A 2006 report by the American Society for Training and Development[96] showed that 70 per cent of training failure could be attributed to lack of follow-up after a training event. This included things like a lack of manager and peer support, no incentive to apply the new lessons and most importantly a lack of the kind of coaching and feedback vital for developing adaptive changes.

CAUSES OF 'TRAINING FAILURE'

Preparation and Readiness (20%)
Learning Intervention (10%)
Application Environment (70%)

As a result of not applying the lessons back on the job, organisations are losing a huge amount of unrealised value.[97]

4. **Failure to understand and measure ROI**

When the training content is too generic and not linked to business objectives, it becomes hard to measure the impact of the training on business drivers. Often there are no performance measurements tied to the training objectives. Instead, in order to close the measurement gap, organisations are forced to rely on fall-back measures like total participant numbers and satisfaction with workshop experience. While these metrics can provide some useful data they are not sufficient for accurately evaluating the desired performance improvements and impact to the business bottom line. This appears to be an exercise in 'ticking the training box' rather than delivering performance outcomes. Valuable dollars are wasted and companies are getting a poor return on their investment.[98]

5. **Investing the learning budget in the wrong place**

Dr. Brent Peterson of Columbia University undertook a study to compare the amount of time spent developing training and related activities, and what actually contributes to learning effectiveness. He found the typical organisation invests 85 per cent of its resources in the training event, yet those events only contributed 24 per cent of the learning effectiveness. Notably, organisations only invest 5 per cent of their time in follow-up, which contributes 50 per cent towards the learning effectiveness. Dr. Peterson's findings are compelling and show the need for organisations to allocate a far greater percentage of their training budgets to on-the-job learning in addition to a training event.

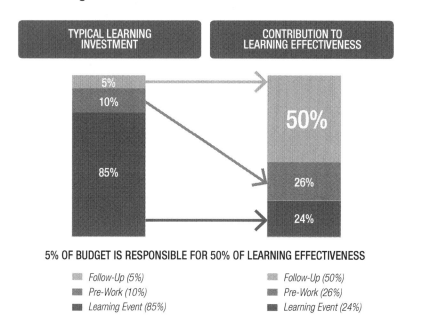

5% OF BUDGET IS RESPONSIBLE FOR 50% OF LEARNING EFFECTIVENESS

- Follow-Up (5%)
- Pre-Work (10%)
- Learning Event (85%)

- Follow-Up (50%)
- Pre-Work (26%)
- Learning Event (24%)

While some organisations are ahead of the game with post-training follow-up, research suggests more work needs to be done.

SUMMARY

- Leadership coaching and training require flexibility.
- There are two types of change: adaptive and technical. Leadership development generally requires adaptive change.
- Five reasons training programs fail: content is loose; formal learning has limited impact; the corporate environment is unsupportive; ROI isn't measured and the budget is directed into the wrong areas.

Performance management is broken

In addition to sending people on training programs, another way organisations tackle leadership development is via the performance management system.

Typically, organisations have an annual performance management conversation to evaluate past performance, determine future direction and agree on strategies to move forward. The effectiveness of performance appraisals is now hotly debated.

"I spoke to my manager once a year about my performance. She said I was doing well, gave me some things to improve and approved a few courses I could do to continue my development. We never talked about the last courses I went on. We never really talked about where my career was heading and what I needed to do to get there. We never talked about challenging projects I could take on within my role to stretch myself. In the end, I left. I just didn't feel supported in my career."

Use-by date reached?

This is a typical comment from our clients. It reflects that performance management conversations have earned a bad reputation, both from those giving them and those receiving them. In Deloitte's global survey[99], only 8 per cent of companies surveyed reported that performance management drives high levels of value. Fifty eight per cent said it was not an effective use of time. Overall ranking/rating-based performance management is perceived as "damaging employee engagement, alienating high performers and costing leaders valuable time."[100] DeNisi and Kluger[101] suggest that only 41 per cent of performance appraisal interventions are effective at improving performance and that 38 per cent of the time, they actually end up making matters worse.

Ticking a box to show you have completed annual performance conversations can provide a false sense that you are developing your people at work. Developing leadership performance is an on-the-ground activity, requiring regular in-the-moment conversations about progress. It's not about filling in a form once a year.

THE SEVEN ESSENTIALS OF LEADERSHIP DEVELOPMENT

If training programs on their own don't deliver, and performance management is broken, how do we close the leadership development gap?

1. We need to formalise informal learning.[102] Organisations need a learning culture within an organisational structure that supports learning.

2. There must be less push and more pull. Performance development must be self-driven to assist the acquisition of the new skills and experiences needed to succeed. According to social cognitive neuroscience, a person's motivation to change and grow is highest when they develop their own insight.[103]

3. Social learning is an important part of knowledge. Learners learn best when they share their expertise with others.[104]

4. Learning is pervasive and takes place outside of the formal learning environment through multiple channels.[105]

5. Learning needs to be personalised and incorporate experience, coaching, observation and feedback. Leaders need to play a key role in the learning process of their people.

6. Companies need to redirect their focus to learning integration on the job to optimise their learning investment.

7. Scrap the annual evaluation cycle and replace it with ongoing feedback and coaching designed to promote continuous employee development.[106]

The process for developing direct reports using the 3D Development Model, has been developed in response to these seven essentials of leadership development. How does developing the leadership of your direct reports, under the direct development model (on the job in a tailored way) compare to standard leadership development?

STANDARD DEVELOPMENT	DIRECT DEVELOPMENT
Formal and outsourced (send on a course)	Informal and on-the-job (encourage range of development options centred around on-job feedback)
Off-the-shelf solution	Targeted solution
Transactional	Transformational
Directive mindset	Coaching mindset
Tell- give the 'solution'	Ask - assist 'exploration'
Parent	Partner
Focus on behaviour	Explore intention driving behaviour
Short term and unsustainable	Long term and sustainable

There is more to developing the leadership potential of your direct reports than occasional training and annual performance conversations alone. There is a delicate ecosystem of mindsets, habits, skills and environmental conditions that must come together to create the conditions that allow leaders to connect their people with their potential.

SUMMARY

- Performance management no longer delivers.
- Seven essentials of leadership development are: informal learning, self-driven learning, social learning, multiple learning channels, personalised learning, increased learning on the job and ongoing feedback replacing annual performance management.
- Direct leadership development delivers.

Final thoughts

Developing direct reports is not a one-size-fits-all approach. Humans are complicated and they don't have a user manual. In this book we have explored the pitfalls of being promoted into leadership roles based on technical skills alone; discussed why the leadership of leaders needs to change; and why being able to develop the leadership skills of your people is vital for engagement, agility and results.

Knowing the issue provides the knowledge for the way forward, and yet it is only the ongoing commitment and action of you, and your direct report that will translate this knowledge into new habits and behaviours. Leadership development through annual performance conversations or one-off training events won't deliver this targeted behaviour change, but your direct development efforts will.

It is the combination of discovering the issue, decoding the intentions and designing the path forward for any of the 12 derailers covered that will take the guesswork out of leading leaders.

We hope this book inspires you to amplify the true potential of your people. It may not be an easy journey, but we promise you, it will be worthwhile.

> *"Often, it's not about becoming a new person, but becoming the person you were meant to be, and already are, but don't know how to be."*
> *Heath L. Buckmaster, Box of Hair: A Fairy Tale*

Notes

Introducton

1. Leslie, J. B., & Van Velsor, E. (1996). A look at derailment today: North America and Europe. Greensboro, NC: Center for Creative Leadership.

2. Orr, J. E. & Sack, K. (2009). Setting the Stage for Success: Building the Leadership Skills that Matter. [White paper]. Retrieved from http://www.kornferry.com/media/lominger_pdf/LA_article_web.pdf.

How best to use this book

3. Orr, J. E. & Sack, K. (2009). Setting the Stage for Success: Building the Leadership Skills that Matter. [White paper]. Retrieved from http://www.kornferry.com/media/lominger_pdf/LA_article_web.pdf.

PART 1 – WHY DEVELOP YOUR DIRECT REPORTS?
Why leadership of leaders needs to change

4. Lieberman, M. (2013, September 19). The social brain and its superpowers: Matthew Lieberman, Ph.D. [TEDx video file]. St. Louis, Missouri, USA: TEDx. Retrieved from https://www.youtube.com/watch?v=NNhk3owF7RQ.

5. McKinsey & Company. (September 2014). Interview: Tom Peters on leading the 21st-century organization.McKinsey.com. Retrieved April 19, 2015 from http://www.mckinsey.com/insights/organization/tom_peters_on_leading_the_21st_century_organization.

6. 1 million people were active on Facebook at 1 December 2004. By 1 December 2009 this number had increased to 360 million people. By 31 December 2014 Facebook statistics reflected 890 million daily active users (average). In Facebook [Company-info page]. Retrieved April 14, 2015 from http://newsroom.fb.com/company-info/.

7. Rousseau, D. (1995). Psychological Contracts in Organizations: Understanding Written and Unwritten Agreements. Thousand Oaks, CA, USA: Sage Publications, Inc.

8. A study found that Harvard MBAs, (on average), change companies three to four times during their first 10 years out of school. See Reichheld, F. F. (2001). Lead for loyalty. Harvard Business Review, 79(7), pp. 76-84.

9. Lockwood, N. R. (2007). Leveraging employee engagement for competitive advantage: HR's strategic role. HR Magazine, 52(3), pp. 1-11.

10. Population growth has led to large numbers of millennials entering the workforce. Simultaneously baby boomers are working longer for financial reasons and for career satisfaction. This has led to the most multi-generational workforce ever seen adding another layer of complexity to achieving employee engagement.

11. Hewitt. (2004). Research brief: Employee engagement higher at double-digit growth companies. Retrieved from http://www.mckpeople.com.au/SiteMedia/w3svc161/Uploads/Documents/016fc140-895a-41bf-90df-9ddb28f4bdab.pdf.

12. Corporate Leadership Council. (2004). Driving performance and retention through employee engagement. Washington, DC, USA: Corporate Executive Board. Retrieved from: http://www.mckpeople.com.au/SiteMedia/w3svc161/Uploads/Documents/760af459-93b3-43c7-b52a-2a74e984c1a0.pdf.

13. Towers Perrin. (2003). Working today: Understanding what drives employee engagement. [White paper]. Retrieved from http://www.keepem.com/doc_files/Towers_Perrin_Talent_2003(TheFinal).pdf.

14. IBM. (2010). Capitalizing on Complexity: Insights from the Global Chief Executive Officer Study. Retrieved from http://public.dhe.ibm.com/common/ssi/ecm/en/gbe03297usen/GBE03297USEN.PDF.

15. Stiehm, J. H., & Townsend, N. W. (2002). The U.S. Army War College: Military Education in a Democracy. Temple University Press.

16. Deloitte Consulting LLP & Bersin by Deloitte. (2014). Global Human Capital Trends: Engaging the 21st-century workforce. [White paper]. Retrieved 14 April 2015 from Deloitte University Press: http://dupress.com/wp-content/uploads/2014/04/GlobalHumanCapitalTrends_2014.pdf.

17. According to Forrester estimates, cloud computing will grow from a $41 billion business in 2011 to a $241 billion business by 2020. Larry Dignan. (April 22, 2011) Cloud computing market: $241 billion in 2020. [Blog post]. Retrieved from http://www.zdnet.com/article/cloud-computing-market-241-billion-in-2020/.

18. Avolio, B. J., Walumbwa, F. O., & Weber, T. J. (2009, January). Leadership: Current Theories, Research, and Future Directions. Annual Reviews, 60,421–449. DOI: 10.1146/annurev.psych.60.110707.163621.

19. Deloitte Consulting LLP and Bersin by Deloitte. (2014). Global Human Capital Trends 2014: Engaging the 21st-century workforce. [White paper]. Retrieved from http://dupress.com/wp-content/uploads/2014/04/GlobalHumanCapitalTrends_2014.pdf. See p.12 of the report for the capability shortfalls by region.

20. Goldsmith, M., with Reiter, M. (2007). What got you here won't get you there: How successful people become even more successful. New York: Hyperion.

21. McCall, M. W., & Lombardo, M. M. (1983, February). What makes a top executive? Psychology Today, 17(2). pp.26-31.

22. The concept derives from a variety of studies conducted at the Center for Creative Leadership.

23. Lombardo, M. M., & Eichinger, R. W. (1989). Preventing derailment: What to do before it's too late. Greensboro, North Carolina: Center for Creative Leadership.

24. Dr Norman Doidge's book, The Brain that Changes Itself' catapulted the concept of neuroplasticity onto the world stage. His engaging collection of stories catalogue our ability to actively exercise our brain to improve functioning, cure deficits and disorders, rejuvenate our brain or recover faculties previously lost including overcoming mental illness and long standing character traits. See: Doidge, N. (2007). The brain that changes itself: Stories of personal triumph from the frontiers of brain science. New York: Viking.

Why developing your direct reports matters

25. Dale Carnegie Training. (2012). Emotional Drivers of Employee Engagement. [White paper]. Retrieved from http://prcounts.com/uploads/Emotional_Drivers_of_Employee_Engagement.pdf.

PART 2 – HOW TO DEVELOP YOUR DIRECT REPORTS
The mindset for developing leadership performance

26. Bersin & Associates/Stacia Sherman Garr. (November 2011). High-Impact Performance Management: Maximizing Performance Coaching. Retrieved from http://marketing.bersin.com/rs/bersin/images/111511_ES_HIPM-Practices1_SSG_Final.pdf.

27. Fundamental attribution error: An identified bias from the discipline of social psychology, the fundamental attribution error, (also known as the correspondence bias or attribution effect), is a person's tendency to place an undue emphasis on internal characteristics to explain someone else's behaviour in a specific context, rather than considering external factors.

28. Rosenthal, R. & Jacobson, L. (1968). Pygmalion in the classroom. New York: Holt, Rinehart & Winston.

29. Rock, D. (2007). Quite Leadership: Six steps to transforming performance at work. New York: Harper Collins. See also Rock D. 2006. A Brain-Based Approach to Coaching. International Journal of Coaching in Organizations, 4(2) pp.32-43.

30. Heath, C., & Heath, D. (2011). Switch: How to change things when change is hard. Waterville, Me: Thorndike Press.

31. Petrie, N. (2011) Future Trends in Leadership Development. [White paper]. Center for Creative Leadership, North Carolina, USA. Retrieved from http://www.ccl.org/Leadership/pdf/research/futureTrends.pdf.

32. Pink, D. H. (2009) Drive: The Surprising Truth About What Motivates Us. New York, NY: Riverhead Books.

33. Rock D. 2006. A Brain-Based Approach to Coaching. International Journal of Coaching in Organizations, 4(2) pp.32-43.

34. Leslie, J. B., & Van Velsor, E. (1996). A look at derailment today: North America and Europe. Greensboro, NC: Center for Creative Leadership. p.11.

Three steps to develop your direct reports

35. Dunning, D., Heath, C., & Suls, J.M. (2004, December) Flawed Self-Assessment – Implications for Health, Education and the Workplace. Psychological Science in the Public Interest 5(3), pp. 69-106. Doi:10.1111/j.1529-1006.2004.00018.x.

36. Kahneman, D. (2011) Thinking, Fast and Slow. New York: NY Macmillan.

37. Zenger, J. & Folkman, J. (2014, January 15,) Re: Your Employees Want the Negative Feedback you Hate to Give. Retrieved from: https://hbr.org/2014/01/your-employees-want-the-negative-feedback-you-hate-to-give/. See also: PsyBlog: (2012, June, 10) The Dunning-Kruger Effect: Why the Incompetent Don't Know They're Incompetent. Retrieved from: http://www.spring.org.uk/2012/06/the-dunning-kruger-effect-why-the-incompetent-dont-know-theyre-incompetent.php.

PART 3 – THE 12 LEADERSHIP DERAILERS
Staller – analysis paralysis

38. Carpenter, M., Bauer, T., Erdogan, B., & Short, J. (2013). Principles of Management, version 1.1. Nyack, NY: Flat World Knowledge.

39. Stibel, J.M. (December 11, 2009). Why Wise Leaders Don't Know Too Much. [Blog post]. Harvard Business Review. Retrieved from https://hbr.org/2009/12/why-wise-leaders-dont-know.

40. Ashkenas, R. (2011, August 16). The Problem with Perfection. [Blog post]. Harvard Business Review. Retrieved from https://hbr.org/2011/08/the-problem-with-perfection.html.

41. Lovegrove, E. (2011, October 24). Zeno's Paper, Or, The Paralysis of Analysis. Retrieved from http://astrobites.org/2011/10/24/zenos-paper-or-the-paralysis-of-analysis/.

Controller – command and control

42. Cuddy, A. J., Kohut, M., & Neffinger, J. (2013, July-August). Connect, Then Lead. Harvard Business Review. Retrieved from https://hbr.org/2013/07/connect-then-lead/ar/.

43. Cuddy, A. J., Kohut, M., & Neffinger, J. (2013, July-August). Connect, Then Lead. Harvard Business Review. Retrieved from https://hbr.org/2013/07/connect-then-lead/ar/

44. Princeton social psychologist Alex Todorov has conducted research into the cognitive and neural mechanisms that drive our spontaneous trait inferences. He found that when we look at each other's faces and make snap judgments we consistently pick up on warmth faster than competence. See Cuddy, A. J., Kohut, M., & Neffinger, J. (2013, July-August). Connect, Then Lead. Harvard Business Review. Retrieved from https://hbr.org/2013/07/connect-then-lead/ar/.

45. Cuddy, A. J., Kohut, M., & Neffinger, J. (2013, July-August). Connect, Then Lead. Harvard Business Review. Retrieved from https://hbr.org/2013/07/connect-then-lead/ar/.

46. Lieberman, M. D. (2013). Social: Why our brains are wired to connect. New York, NY: Crown.

47. Eisenberger, N. & Kohlrieser, G. (2012, November 16) Lead with your Heart, Not Just your Head. [Blog post]. Harvard Business Review. Retrieved from https://hbr.org/2012/11/are-you-getting-personal-as-a/.

48. Lieberman, M. D. (2013). Social: Why our brains are wired to connect. New York, NY: Crown.

Cyclone – bull at a gate

49. Stenger, M. (2013, December 30). Haste Makes Waste: New study indicates the brain is less accurate when under speed stress. [Blog post]. Retrieved from http://www.opencolleges.edu.au/informed/news/brain-less-accurate-when-under-speed-stress/#ixzz3lzOvjpt7.

50. Kahneman, D. (2011). Thinking Fast and Slow. New York: NY MacMillan.

51. Rockwell, D. (2011, July 29). Overcoming the Six Dangers of Flip-Flopping. Retrieved from Leadership Freak: http://leadershipfreak.wordpress.com/2011/07/29/overcoming-the-six-dangers-of-flip-flopping/.

Doer – can't delegate

52. Mackay, H. (2012, October 12). 6 Ways to Delegate more effectively. [Blog post]. Retrieved from http://www.inc.com/harvey-mackay/6-keys-effective-delegation.html.

53. Gallo, A. (2012, July 26) Why aren't you delegating? [Blog post]. Retrieved from http://blogs.hbr.org/2012/07/why-arent-you-delegating/.

54. Birkinshaw, J. & Cohen, J. (2013, September). Make time for Work That Matters. Harvard Business Review, 91(9), 115-118.

Avoider – conflict averse

55. Senge, P. (1990) The Fifth Discipline: The Art & Practice of the Learning Organization. London: UK Random House p.249.

56. Kohlrieser, G. (2006). Hostage at the Table: How Leaders can Overcome Conflict, Influence Others, and Raise Performance. San Francisco, CA: Jossey-Bass. p.100.

57. Kohlrieser, G. (2006). Hostage at the Table: How Leaders can Overcome Conflict, Influence Others, and Raise Performance. San Francisco, CA: Jossey-Bass. p.100.

58. Kohlrieser, G. (2006). Hostage at the Table: How Leaders can Overcome Conflict, Influence Others, and Raise Performance. San Francisco, CA: Jossey-Bass. pp.152-154.

59. Kohlrieser, G. (2006). Hostage at the Table: How Leaders can Overcome Conflict, Influence Others, and Raise Performance. San Francisco, CA: Jossey-Bass. p.152.

60. Kohlrieser, G. (2006). Hostage at the Table: How Leaders can Overcome Conflict, Influence Others, and Raise Performance. San Francisco, CA: Jossey-Bass. p.154.

61. Kohlrieser, G. (2006). Hostage at the Table: How Leaders can Overcome Conflict, Influence Others, and Raise Performance. San Francisco, CA: Jossey-Bass. p.154.

Fence-sitter – indecisive leader

62. Heath, C., & Heath, D. (2013). Decisive: How to make better choices in life and work. New York: Crown Business.

63. Arsham, Prof. H., (1994) Leadership Decision Making [on line article – 8th ed.]. Retrieved from the University of Baltimore http://home.ubalt.edu/ntsbarsh/opre640/partxiii.htm#rhowtoavoid.

64. Danzige, S., Levav, J., & Avnaim-Pesso, L. (2011). Extraneous factors in judicial decisions. PNAS, 108(17), 6889-6892. Retrieved from http://www.pnas.org/content/108/17/6889.full.pdf.

65. Heath, C., & Heath, D. (2013). Decisive: How to make better choices in life and work. New York: Crown Business.

Know-it-all – closed to other ideas

66. Kahneman, D. (2011). Thinking Fast and Slow. New York: NY MacMillan.

67. Kahneman, D. (2011). Thinking Fast and Slow. New York: NY MacMillan. p.28.

68. Mezirow, J. (2000). Learning to Think Like An Adult: Core Concepts of Transformation Theory. In J. Mezirow & Associates, Learning as Transformation: Critical perspectives on a theory in progress (p. 4). San Francisco: Jossey-Bass.

69. Hess, E. D. (2014). Learn or Die: Using Science to Build a Leading-Edge Learning Organization (Kindle ed.) Columbia Business School Publishing.

Guardian – inability to innovate

70. Reference for Business: Encyclopaedia of Business, (2nd ed.). Retrieved from http://www.referenceforbusiness.com/encyclopedia/Inc-Int/Innovation.html.

71. Dyer, J. H., Gregersen, H., & Christensen, C. M. (2009, December 1). The Innovator's DNA. Retrieved from Harvard Business Review: https://hbr.org/2009/12/the-innovators-dna.

72. Baumgartner, J. (n.d). What is Innovative Leadership? [Blog post]. Retrieved from Innovation Management.se: http://www.innovationmanagement.se/imtool-articles/what-is-innovative-leadership/.

Micromanager – management on a leash

73. Collins, S. K., Collins, K. S. (2002, November). Micromanagement – a costly management style. Retrieved October 13, 2014, from Pubfacts Scientific Publication Data: http://www.pubfacts.com/detail/12510608/Micromanagement--a-costly-management-style.

74. James, C. (2014, January 21). How to manage a micro manager. The Sydney Morning Herald. Retrieved November 13, 2014, from http://www.smh.com.au/small-business/managing/how-to-manage-a-micro-manager-20131211-2z5cx.html. Study of 2223 professionals.

75. Wagner. R., & Harter Ph.D, J. K. (2006, November 1) 12: The Elements of Great Managing (1 ed.). Washington, D.C.: Gallup Press.

76. Mind Tools. (n.d.). Avoiding Micromanagement. Mindtools.com. Retrieved from http://www.mindtools.com/pages/article/newTMM_90.htm.

Poker face – showing no emotion

77. Condeluci, A. (n.d.). Communication & Leadership. Mamre.org.au. Retrieved from https://www.

mamre.org.au/sites/mamre.org.au/files/docs/AlCondeluci/Monographs/Communication%20and%20 Leadership.pdf.

78. Harvard Business Publishing. (2008, August 11). Social Intelligence and Leadership [video file]. Retrieved from http://www.youtube.com/watch?v=7Qv0o1oh9f4.

79. Lieberman, M. D. (2013) Social: Why our brains are wired to connect. New York, NY: Crown.

80. McAleer P, Todorov A, Belin P (2014) How Do You Say 'Hello'? Personality Impressions from Brief Novel Voices. PLoS ONE 9(3): e90779. doi:10.1371/journal.pone.0090779.

81. Goman Ph.D. C. K. (2011). The Silent Language of Leaders: How Body Language Can Help—or Hurt— How You Lead. California, US: Jossey-Bass.

People burner – poor people skills

82. Lieberman, M. (2013, December 27). Should Leaders Focus on Results, or on People? Retrieved from Harvard Business Review: https://hbr.org/2013/12/should-leaders-focus-on-results-or-on-people.

83. Harvard Business Publishing. (2008, August 11). Social Intelligence and Leadership [video file]. Retrieved from http://www.youtube.com/watch?v=7Qv0o1oh9f4.

84. Goleman, D., & Boyatzis, R. E. (2008, September 1). Social Intelligence and the Biology of Leadership. Retrieved from Harvard Business Review: https://hbr.org/2008/09/social-intelligence-and-the-biology-of-leadership.

85. Goleman, D., & Boyatzis, R. E. (2008, September 1). Social Intelligence and the Biology of Leadership. Retrieved from Harvard Business Review: https://hbr.org/2008/09/social-intelligence-and-the-biology-of-leadership.

86. Goleman, D., (2006). Emotional intelligence: why it can matter more that IQ. (10th anniversary ed.). New York: NY Bantam Books.

Tactician – poor strategic thinker

87. Schoemaker, P. J., Krupp, S., & Howland, S. (2013, January 1). Strategic Leadership: The Essential Skills. Retrieved from Harvard Business Review http://hbr.org/2013/01/strategic-leadership-the-esssential-skills/ar/1.

88. Five iterations of asking why is generally sufficient to get to a root cause. The technique was originally developed by Sakichi Toyoda and was used within the Toyota Motor Corporation during the evolution of its manufacturing methodologies.

PART 4 – MORE ON THE IMPERATIVE TO CHANGE LEADERSHIP DEVELOPMENT RIGHT NOW

Developing direct reports requires new thinking

89. Heifetz, R. A., & Laurie, D.L. (1997). The Work of Leadership. Harvard Business Review, Jan-Feb 75(1),pp. 124-34.

90. Heiftez, R. A. & Linsky, M. (2002) Leadership on the Line: Staying Alive through the Dangers of Leading. Boston, Massachusetts: Harvard Business Review Press p.14.

91. Petrie, N. (2011, August). Future Trends in Leadership Development [White paper p.10]. ccl.org. Retrieved from http://www.ccl.org/Leadership/pdf/research/futureTrends.pdf.

92. 1975: Percentage of formal learning that is actually applied to the job: 15%. 2005: Percentage of formal learning that is actually applied to the job: 15%. Robinson,D. (2008). Performance Consulting 2.0: What's the same and What's different. Paper presented at the Association for Talent Development International Conference & Expo. Retrieved from http://astd2008.astd.org/PDF/Speaker%20

Handouts/ice08%20handout%20M202.pdf.

93. Horwitch, M., & Whipple, M. (2014, June 11). Leaders who inspire: A 21st Century approach to developing your talent. [White paper] Retrieved from http://www.bain.com/publications/articles/leaders-who-inspire.aspx.

94. Petrie, N. (2011, August). Future Trends in Leadership Development [White paper p.10]. ccl.org. Retrieved from http://www.ccl.org/Leadership/pdf/research/futureTrends.pdf.

95. Kirkpatrick Ph.D., J., & Kirkpatrick, W. K. (2009, April). The Kirkpatrick Four Levels: A Fresh Look After 50 Years 1959-2009. [White paper]. See pp.5. Retrieved from http://www.kirkpatrickpartners.com/Portals/0/Resources/Kirkpatrick%20Four%20Levels%20white%20paper.pdf.

96. 1975: Percentage of formal learning that is actually applied to the job: 15%. 2005: Percentage of formal learning that is actually applied to the job: 15%. Robinson,D. (2008). Performance Consulting 2.0: What's the same and What's different. Paper presented at the Association for Talent Development International Conference & Expo. Retrieved from http://astd2008.astd.org/PDF/Speaker%20Handouts/ice08%20handout%20M202.pdf.

97. Brinkerhoff R, O., (2012), Maximising the value of Learning and Development. [PowerPoint slides]. Retrieved April 19, 2015 from: https://www.timetag.tv/content/learningtechnologies/18184/18666_slides.pdf.

98. Brinkerhoff R, O., (2012), Maximising the value of Learning and Development. [PowerPoint slides]. Retrieved April 19, 2015 from: https://www.timetag.tv/content/learningtechnologies/18184/18666_slides.pdf.

Performance management is broken

99. Barry, L., Erhardt-Lewis, A., & Liakopoulos, A. (2014).Global Human Capital Trends 2014: Engaging the 21st-century workforce. [White paper] p.45-47 Retrieved from Deloitte University Press: http://www.deloitte.com/assets/Dcom-Namibia/GlobalHumanCapitalTrends2014_030714.pdf.

100. Barry, L., Erhardt-Lewis, A., & Liakopoulos, A. (2014).Global Human Capital Trends 2014: Engaging the 21st-century workforce. [White paper] p.45-47 Retrieved from Deloitte University Press: http://www.deloitte.com/assets/Dcom-Namibia/GlobalHumanCapitalTrends2014_030714.pdf.

101. DeNisi, A. S., & Kluger, A. N. (2000, February 1). Feedback effectiveness: Can 360-degree appraisals be improved?Perspectives, 14(1). doi:10.5465/AME.2000.2909845

102. Bersin, J. (2009, May). Modern Corporate Training: Formalize Informal Learning. [PowerPoint slides]. Retrieved October 25, 2014 from http://www.cedma-europe.org/newsletter%20articles/Webinars/Formalizing%20Informal%20Learning%20(May%202009).pdf.

103. Rock, D. (2006). A Brain-Based Approach to Coaching. International Journal of Coaching in Organizations. 4(2), pp.32-32

104. Lieberman, M.D. (2013) Social: Why our brains are wired to connect. New York, NY: Crown p.289

105. Rayson, S. (2013).Learning at the need of speed: Top 10 tasks for L&D in 2014. [White paper]. Retrieved from http://www.kineo.com/resources/papers-and-guides/learning-strategy-and-design/learning-insights-report-2013.

106. Barry, L., Erhardt-Lewis, A., & Liakopoulos, A. (2014).Global Human Capital Trends 2014: Engaging the 21st-century workforce. [White paper] p.45-47 Retrieved from Deloitte University Press: http://www.deloitte.com/assets/Dcom-Namibia/GlobalHumanCapitalTrends2014_030714.pdf.

Index

A

accountability, 45, 64, 88, 129, 142, 145, 185

action, taking, 8, 11, 29, 35, 43, 45, 48, 58, 59, 72, 76, 77, 79, 100–103, 105, 106, 137, 146, 159, 220, 224

adaptability, 23, 26, 41, 48, 75, 156, 158, 237–240

American Society for Training and Development, 240

analysis paralysis, 69, 73, 76, 77–78

Arshan, Dr Hossein, 143

Ashkenas, Ron, 76

Australian Employee Engagement Survey, 182

Australian Institute of Management Victoria and Tasmania, 182

autonomy, 175, 180,

B

biases, 54, 56
    anchoring, 158
    availability, 158
    cognitive, 42, 104
    confirmation, 104, 157
    self-interest, 158
    superiority illusion, 158

Birkinshaw, Julian, 117–118

body language, 192, 193–194, 196–198, 204, 210

    see also nonverbal communication

brain, 20, 27–28, 45, 46, 47, 49, 58, 69, 77, 90, 103–104, 131, 143, 157, 168, 195, 209, 224

    see also neural pathways; neuroplasticity

Buechner, Carl W, 210

bullying, 86–88, 204

C

Center for Creative Leadership, 8, 47, 48

coaching, 14, 41, 44–45, 56, 63–65, 83, 86, 154, 246

    see also Coaching Tips

Coaching Tips, 77, 91, 105, 118, 133, 145, 158, 170, 183, 197, 210, 223

    see also coaching

cognitive dissonance, 157

Cohen, Jordan, 117–118

collaboration, 25, 49, 89, 92, 116, 146, 185, 196, 211

Columbia University, 241

commitment, 46, 48, 83, 86, 158, 220, 223, 251

communication, 90, 102, 130, 189, 192–195, 197–199, 206

conceptual thinking, 101, 103, 105, 215, 219, 220, 223–224, 226 confidence, 21, 141, 155, 156, 159–160, 231

conflict, 116, 125, 128–135

consensus, 20, 88, 114, 144, 155

context, 25, 27, 41, 46, 49, 50, 53, 59, 63, 74, 101, 181, 195, 220

control, 83, 87–92, 115–116, 121, 179, 181, 185, 197, 207

   see also power

Covey, Stephen, 8

Cuddy, Amy, 90

D

decision fatigue, 143, 144, 147

decision-making, 46, 48, 56, 72–80, 102–107, 137, 140–147, 154–155, 157, 158–159, 183, 209, 223

Decisive (Heath), 143

delegation, 87, 88, 89, 91, 92–93, 109, 112–122, 147, 180, 181, 206

Deloitte study, 26, 245

DeNisi, AS, 245

derailers, leadership, 49, 55, 67–227

   avoider, 125–135

   controller, 83–94

   cyclone, 97–107

   doer, 109–122

   fence-sitter, 137–148

   guardian, 163–173

   know-it-all, 151–160

   micromanager, 175–187

   people burner, 201–213

   poker face, 189–199

   staller, 69–80

   tactician, 215–227

details, significance of, 69, 75, 79, 88, 91–92, 115, 119–120, 121, 180, 184, 221, 226

development conversations, 8, 9, 11, 14, 58, 63, 233

direct reports, development of, 21–29, 53–60

   coaching of, 63–65

   factors for success, 49–50

   fundamental mindsets, 48

   key principles to develop, 41–47

   Performance Development ladder, The, 33–36

   3D Development Model, 53–59

directive, 20, 88, 90, 115, 181

Dyer, JH, 169

E

Eisenberger, Naomi, 90

emotional intelligence, 47, 195, 207, 208

empathy, 130, 132, 134, 195, 196, 206, 210

environment, changing, 23, 24, 26, 47, 59, 163, 167, 169

F

feedback, importance of, 28, 35, 41, 48, 55, 59, 178, 240, 246

Fifth Discipline, The (Senge), 131

flexibility, 22, 28, 87, 159, 220

G

Ghandi, 93–94

Give and Take (Grant), 209

Gleeson, Tony, 182

globalisation, 23, 26

Goldsmith, Marshall, 232

Golem effect, 43

Goleman, Daniel, 195, 208

Grant, Dr Adam, 209–210

H

Harvard Business Review, 76, 90, 197, 208, 222

Heath, Chip and Dan, 46, 143, 146

Heiftez, RA, 238

Hess, Edward, 157–158

heuristics, 157

Hostage at the Table: How Leaders Can Overcome Conflict, Influence Others, and Raise Performance (Kohlrieser), 131

I

innovation, 42, 49, 86, 163, 166–173

Institute for Corporate Productivity, 116

J

Johns Hopkins Carey Business School, 143

K

Kahneman, Daniel, 28, 104, 156–157

Kinsey Goman, Carol, 196–197

Kluger, AN, 245

Kohlrieser, George, 131–132

Kohut, Matthew, 90

Krause, Tom, 212

L

Leadership Decision Making (Arshan), 143

leadership development, 28, 41, 57, 59, 63, 232, 237–243, 245–248, 251

    direct development model, 247

    seven essentials, 246

    standard development model, 247

Learn or Die (Hess), 157

Lieberman, Matthew, 19, 90, 195, 208

Linsky, M, 238

London Business School, 117

Lovegrove, Elizabeth, 77

M

McAleer, Dr Phil, 196

market trends, 221, 225–226

Mezirow, Jack, 157

micromanagement, 115, 175, 178–186

MindTools, 182

motivation, importance of 28, 43, 54, 57, 155, 169, 170, 246

N

National Academy of Sciences, 144

Neffinger, John, 90

negotiation, 129, 131, 132, 133

neural pathways/connections, 20, 28, 47, 58

   see also brain

neuroplasticity, 20, 27–28, 47

   see also brain

neuroscience, 246

   see also brain

nonverbal communication, 194–199, 205, 206, 210

   see also body language

O

observer-expectancy effect, 104

P

'Paralysis by Analysis' (Lovegrove), 77

Pareto principle, 119, 184

Penney, James Cash, 116

people skills, 35, 201, 206–207, 210–212

perfectionism, 74, 142, 145, 181, 186

performance conversations, 46, 64, 246, 247, 251

Performance Development Ladder, 33–36

performance management, 229, 245–247

personal achievement, 89, 92, 115, 120

Peterson, Dr Brent, 241

power, 83, 86, 87, 89, 93–94, 156

   see also control

productivity, 78, 89, 109, 112, 113, 117, 121, 175, 179, 180, 182, 206, 207, 209

psychologists, 90, 144, 196

   see also psychology

psychology, 22, 43, 89, 131

   see also psychologists

Pygmalion effect, 43

Q

Quiet Leadership: Six Steps to Transforming Performance at Work (Rock), 44

R

Reagan, Ronald, 133

Reference for Business: Encyclopaedia of Business, 169

responsibility, taking, 21, 45, 47, 87, 88–89, 91, 92, 116, 117, 121, 142, 145, 183, 184, 185, 226

risks, taking, 50, 73, 75, 77, 86, 101–103, 105, 130, 131, 142, 145, 163, 167, 168, 169, 171, 186, 220

Rock, David, 44

Rockwell, Dan, 104

role model, 204, 231–232

S

self-awareness, 21, 55–56, 208

self-control, 212

self-identity, 49

self-referencing, 155–156

Senge, Peter, 131

Silent Language of Leaders, The (Kinsey Goman), 196

social cognition, 207, 211-212, 246

social intelligence, 195, 207, 208

social learning, 246

social pain, 90

social skills, 19–20, 207, 208, 212–213

Social: Why Our Brains Are Wired to Connect (Lieberman), 19

Stibel, Jeff, 76

'Strategic Leadership: The Essential Skills', 222

strategic thinking, 219–227

Switch (Heath), 46

T

Thinking Fast and Slow (Kahneman), 156

3D Development Model, 53, 59, 247

Todorov, Alex, 90

transactional, 196

transformational, 20, 157, 196

Twelve: The Elements of Great Managing, 182

U

University of Baltimore, 143

University of Pennsylvania, 209

V

values, 35, 49, 57, 142, 146, 147

Vanderbilt University, 103

Voice Neurocognition Laboratory, 196

W

warmth, 87, 89–90, 93, 196, 206, 210

Wharton School and Decision Strategies International, 222

Welch, Jack, 7

Wild Card coaching tips, 229–233

Wooden, John, 105

Work Less, Do More (Yager), 117

work-life balance, 115, 181, 206

Y

Yager, Jan, 117

Printed in Australia
AUOC02n0849091215
272327AU00004B/4/P

9 780994 260116